BRAVE ENOUGH
NOT TO QUIT

BRAVE ENOUGH
NOT TO QUIT

How I Realised My Football Dream

MILLIE
FARROW

With Katie Field

First published by Pitch Publishing, 2023

Pitch Publishing
9 Donnington Park,
85 Birdham Road,
Chichester,
West Sussex,
PO20 7AJ
www.pitchpublishing.co.uk
info@pitchpublishing.co.uk

A CIP catalogue record is available for this book
from the British Library.

ISBN 978 1 80150 479 9

Typesetting and origination by Pitch Publishing
Printed and bound in Great Britain by TJ Books, Padstow

Contents

Introduction

THE DAY couldn't have been any more perfect. It was 6 May 2012 and I was in the Chelsea team to play against Arsenal in the FA Youth Cup Final. The vibe with the girls was buzzing as always. Everyone was so excited to play, the coaches were in such good spirits. What a day this could be to remember …

But, in the second half I went to intercept a pass (there was no one around me) and the leg that I landed on hyperextended I felt a kind of crack or pop in my knee and I'm sure I heard it too. I instantly went down to the ground and screamed the whole stadium down. Picture a practically empty stadium which usually holds 30,000 people, echoing with my distress. The entire place fell silent …

The pain was horrible. Obviously, something I had never felt before. I was scared, I was worried, what could it have been? I got taken into the changing rooms where my physio did some tests. I had no idea what was going on to be honest, I was so young and clueless. All I cared about was watching my team. All I wanted was for us to win. I was due to go to the hospital, but I refused to go until after the game because I needed to watch my team.

* * *

It was January 2020 and I was playing for Reading in an FA Cup game against a team in the league below us. I was excited to be starting the game but something just didn't really feel right; I know how it feels to be excited to play and this feeling just wasn't the same.

In recent weeks I had been struggling with my anxiety due to relationship reasons, so my head hadn't been in the right place for a while. Almost like an 'I give up' feeling and it really showed during the game.

It started fine. When you play in a team, you get voices coming from everywhere. From the bench, the management area and of course the voices in your head. During the game I could feel myself falling to pieces mentally. I got 'the breathing thing' which hadn't happened to me for a long time. I then lost control of my thoughts. Everything that entered my head was negative.

I saw my parents in the crowd and I nearly burst into tears, wondering what they thought of this shit show. But I kept pulling myself through.

The whistle blew: we had won the game with ease, but it just felt horrible. I was trying to hold in every emotion I was feeling inside and when the team talk had finished, I went straight over to my parents and broke down in their arms, properly crying.

Why did I feel like that? I hate myself for feeling that way. I was embarrassed.

* * *

It was 2022. I had just left Leicester and signed for Crystal Palace. Once again, I was trying to settle in with a new team. I was moving house, and my relationship was coming to an end. I could feel I was mentally losing myself and was struggling. It started to affect my football again. It took me a while to settle in and adjust to the differences.

What do you do when you have no idea why you're feeling a certain way? What do you do when you find yourself losing weight and you can't eat properly because you feel sick due to the horrible thoughts that are entering your head? When you have no motivation but you have to turn up to football and act like you care when all you want to do is curl up in a ball in bed.

I couldn't keep going on like this, keep being caught out by it when I least expected it. It was now or never. My mum had to contact the doctors for me because I couldn't even speak down the phone to them. I was in such a state. I was prescribed Sertraline, an anti-depressant which is commonly used to help anxiety and OCD. I would have taken anything to feel a bit better at this point. I needed to get out of this pit.

* * *

I used to avoid things, or certain people, that would set off my OCD, because I couldn't stand the hassle of listening to my thoughts. I would just avoid a lot of situations that would trigger it.

As an athlete naturally we put ourselves under pressure and I feel that this had a large effect on the severity of my OCD. When I was younger, I used to get so worked up before going on an England camp my OCD would go through the roof leading up to it and during it. When I got home, I used to be so mentally drained. My mind would never rest, it was 24/7 constant stress and worry. This is no way to live.

The outbursts could lead to punching walls, crying my eyes out hysterically, shouting 'fuck off' to my OCD at the top of my voice because I couldn't handle it. I couldn't handle how it made me feel. I just wanted it to go away.

* * *

My name is Millie Farrow and I have been a professional football player since the age of 19. It is likely that you don't know who I am. But you don't need to know who I am for me to take you on this journey.

The fact that I haven't even touched certain levels or dreams of mine in football yet made me debate whether I should write this book, whether people would listen or be interested in what a female professional footballer has to say. But after a lot of thought I've decided that it is best for me to get this out there as soon as possible because I am determined to help others. Not just people in sports but regular everyday people as well, as I feel there are many people out there who can relate to a lot of the messages that lie in my book.

I want to write this book to help people understand that to achieve what we want to achieve in life will always come with incredibly challenging moments and times when you feel the pressure or doubt is never-ending, but if you push through, trust the process and be very patient and persistent, along the way you will learn amazing things about yourself and life itself, if you pay true attention. It is important to understand that there is no end goal.

I am hoping that sharing my story will help people see that going through the hardest of times will only make you stronger in ways you didn't even know or realise and enable you to deal with similar situations a lot better than before, simply from looking at circumstances differently and having a widened perspective. Our mindset is everything.

As a professional footballer I think we all have an idea of what we want to achieve during our career. Even before being a full-time female footballer existed as a career option, I knew it was what I wanted to be. We all have dreams as children. I wanted to play for my country when I was younger. I've always said to myself that I want to get to the highest level in football that I can.

To many people it may sound ridiculous but the injuries and the mental health issues that I have experienced have contributed massively to me getting to where I am now and will also help me on the way to where I eventually end up. My understanding of my mental health problems has seriously opened my eyes and taken me down paths I never imagined I would have to go down.

I want to be living proof of somebody that has been at the lowest point of their career/life and prove that you can hit rock bottom in so many ways but still get yourself back out there achieving and – most importantly – being happy. We are what we believe we are. I am determined to become successful for the aspiring younger kid reading this who may not believe in themselves, or maybe for someone who is going through a tough injury or a tough point in their life and can't see the light at the end of the tunnel.

In the First Half of this book, I take you through my career, in the Second Half I talk about everything I have learned, and in Extra Time I have a chat to Emile Heskey and Fran Kirby – two extremely successful footballers who have overcome problems of their own to reach the top in their careers.

Throughout this book I will open up to the deepest level. Many people will not have experienced some of the things I will be talking about, but I feel there are many people that my experiences will resonate with, and that makes it so important to me.

Life's a journey and it isn't always what it seems at face value.

I will forever be grateful for my struggle because I am convinced it is the reason I keep going, keep wanting to achieve, keep wanting to better myself. It has helped me become so much more aware of many circumstances that are forever changing.

If you are strong enough not to give in to your struggles, I promise you, you will learn in abundance along the way.

Everybody's journey starts somewhere, and this book focuses on my football journey but not the type of journey that you may imagine it to be: this book isn't about trophies, medals, cups, or achievements in the game. This is a football story without the standard glamour that being a footballer may be associated with.

This is me, stripped down to the most vulnerable version of myself.

THE FIRST HALF

Chapter One

The Love for Football Begins

I WAS a very hectic child, always had a lot of energy and showed a lot of interest in any kind of physical activity. My mum Nikki has a few stories to tell about my childhood which give an insight into the kind of person I am. Over to you, Mum ...

'From a very early age it was quite apparent that Millie wasn't going to be a girlie type of girl; she was very certain about the way she wanted to dress which didn't include dresses or anything pink or stereotypically female. There were many occasions when she had been to play round our neighbour's house with her sons and came home dressed in their clothes.

'Millie liked rough and tumble, muck, mud and anything which was extreme in danger, which resulted in many visits to the hospital with fractured collarbones and even a broken ankle. There were many heart-stopping moments when I would look out of the window to see her flying off the 6ft garden wall, landing on the trampoline with a somersault to the ground or climbing up trees, or balancing on the top of climbing frames. So, it wasn't really surprising when I enrolled her into ballet classes that she would sit at the front of the class in her pretty pink tutu with a face like thunder refusing to join in!

'Millie was always playing the fool and wanted to be the centre of attention – she could always bring a smile to anyone's face and still does. There were many occasions when I found myself waiting in the ladies' toilets for Millie, while she sat on the toilet singing at the top of her voice. I would stand outside with an embarrassed look on my face, telling her to hurry up. It did make people smile though!

'Being an escape artist was another talent of Millie's; when her brother Ollie went for a taster day at his new school which was across the road from where we lived, we came home with some of the other parents while we waited. After a while we noticed Millie was no longer in the garden with the other children. Panic started to rise as she could be found nowhere. We checked the street outside and just as I thought I needed to phone the police, a receptionist from the school came to my house and said, "We've found your daughter with an apple playing in the playground on one of the tricycles with her brother."

'She had decided she didn't want to miss out, so let herself out of the house and climbed over the school fence into the playground; hence, soon afterwards, a bolt was installed at the top of our front door. Alas, this was not going to stop her as a few weeks later my neighbour's mum found her round the back of our house trying to climb back over the fence. She definitely kept us on our toes.

'It was when my sister's son started playing football for a local team and invited Millie along to the training sessions, we realised that actually this was the direction in which she wanted to go. Millie would come home covered in mud absolutely buzzing with joy and, from reports from the coaches, she showed great talent.'

My dad Keith also has some memories from my childhood to share.

'Right from the start it was clear that Millie was going to be a live-wire. She was born at breakneck speed and spent the next few months not sleeping much and keeping us awake. At the time we were living in a two-bedroom house, and with our son Ollie in the second bedroom there was no hiding place.

'As she grew, she showed a great interest in games and sport, and had no interest in any matters girly! She loved ball games in particular, football, cricket and tennis amongst her favourites. She was the classic tomboy, and also established herself as the family comedian, a position held to this day.

'I remember one Christmas when her grandma bought her (in error) a make-up bust so she could learn some beauty skills. Upon opening it she looked disgusted and hurled it across the room in anger. Luckily everyone saw the funny side, and to Millie's delight her birthday present from my parents was a musical skeleton. This went down really well and over time a collection of them was amassed.

'She was also quite artful and once when her brother had lost a tooth, the following morning he was happy to find a 20p coin under his pillow. This was strange, as the tooth fairy had actually left a £1 coin there, which had been strangely substituted by you know who during the night!

'Millie genuinely seemed to enjoy her school years and always got involved in a wide variety of activities as well as sports. She started learning to play the violin, much to the delight of my dad who had played to a good level during his formative years. It is said that it takes ten years to play a good note on a fiddle – we never got to hear one, however, and, perhaps fortunately, Millie's career only spanned a year or so before it ebbed away along with the neighbourhood cats!

'My mum is a long-standing member of a choir which for a number of years during the noughties put on a Christmas panto/performance in a local community centre. This offered singing/dancing/acting parts for children aged five and over, and consequently all of our children took their place on the stage when the time came. Millie enjoyed these performances although suffered the wrath of the lady director for talking/ messing about during the rehearsals. She showed no signs of stage fright and had a great time.'

I always had a love for football and my journey in the game started at nine years old, when I was given the opportunity to go and train with the boys' team my cousin was in. As you may know, many female footballers of this generation began playing football with boys, or for a boys' team. Of course, back then there weren't many girls' teams to join, so playing with boys was how many females that now play professionally today started their career.

Not long after I started training with AFC Portchester (my cousin's team), my auntie saw an advert in the local *Sports Mail* for a girls' team called Cosham Blues that was starting up, and they were looking for players. Of course, she told my mum about it and not long afterwards, I was on my way to training.

My dad took me to the session, which took place in a big field in Portsmouth. I was so excited; all that mattered to me was doing well in the session and enjoying myself. The pitches were and still are terrible, but back then I didn't know any different and I didn't really care. All I cared about was being able to play football. Little did anyone know that a young innocent girl was about to start the most incredible journey of her life.

At that first Friday evening training session, I just went out and played. I played my heart out. The training session started, and it was a very strange place for me to be at such a young age – still only nine. My memory isn't as good as my dad's on how the evening went but he told me that the majority of the parents couldn't believe their eyes – they couldn't believe a little girl could play like this. One of them even said, 'She has been sent from heaven', while another one compared me to George Best! They thought I was some brilliant player that had come out of nowhere, but the reality of the situation was that they had just never seen a little girl play football with any ability.

The session came to an end and the manager immediately presented me with the playing kit and confirmed that she could get me registered in time for the game on Sunday, just two days away. Me and Dad got back into the car and as soon as I shut the door I burst into tears because I was so happy, I couldn't believe it. It was an incredible feeling. I was only nine and that's what it meant. Everything. That feeling for football is one that has stayed with me throughout my career so far. The shirt number I got given was four and for many years after that it was my favourite number.

Despite being a girls' team, we were entered in a boys' league, which was obviously very tough and we lost nearly every game. But this was the start for me, the hunger to get to the next level, to score more goals than the game before.

Football wasn't the only sport I was good at as a child. My dad remembers me winning a lot of athletics races. 'At secondary school she managed to break the record for the 800m in years seven, eight, nine and ten,' he says. 'As there was no year 11 sports day there was not the opportunity to complete the clean sweep, although she did help with the organisation of the event for the younger students. This day was to reveal a different quality in Millie's personality that was recognised and commented upon by her then PE teacher Miss Chaplin. The 800m race for year ten had started and it was evident that one runner was capable of beating Millie's record. Some in her position would be hoping that she would fall short, but not Millie who ran around actively encouraging her to succeed, which she duly did.

'Because of her success in football Millie became one of those sporting heroes amongst her peers; every school year across the country has at least one and we all remember their names in respect of our own years. She would beat almost everyone at almost anything, often qualifying for the next level, the inter-school competition.

'At around age 14 she wiped the floor with her year group at cross country, and as a result qualified for the Hampshire schools' qualifiers. Everyone at school was telling her that she was unbeatable and would triumph at what was an elite level. The reality was somewhat different however, as at this level there were kids concentrating on distance running and gaining momentum in their specialised field. The field set off with Millie at the front before disappearing into woodland on a circuit course. We all waited in anticipation by the finish line for the returning runners. Millie was not amongst the leaders and finished well down the field to massive personal disappointment.

'This day revealed a hint of future problems for Millie. She had struggled to breathe properly during the race and in time we came to realise that this was caused by anxiety.

After the race we assured her that the result didn't matter, and I think she accepted this.'

That breathing problem my dad talked about had already happened in some of my football matches, but it took a few years for us to realise I was actually having panic attacks. As my love for football had begun to get stronger, so had the emotions that I experienced. With my desire to succeed growing, this started to influence me mentally. When I was as young as ten, I had my first panic attack, or as I used to call it, 'the breathing thing' – that is what I named it when I tried to explain what was happening to my parents. The first time it happened was during a game. I can't remember exactly what caused it, but I can remember how horrible it was to try and deal with when I had absolutely no idea what was going on. My throat felt like it had closed up and I couldn't breathe properly. As a kid, this was scary and the start of the unknown.

I would get myself very worked up before and during games and end up in tears. It got to a point where my mum took me to see a doctor as we did not understand why it kept happening and I got prescribed an inhaler. Obviously back then I really had no idea why it kept happening and I was unable to explain it to a doctor, which must have led them to believe that an inhaler was the solution. They obviously thought it was a physical illness when the truth is, this was the start of my anxiety problem, and the inhaler wasn't going to do anything to help.

This wasn't something that was going away: it started to happen quite regularly in matches or during any kind of 'important' occasion in sport. Maybe this was the beginning of me putting pressure on myself, the start of trying to be a perfectionist. I always wanted to do well in everything I did, but when it came to football, it was and is another level. I had ridiculously high expectations of myself from as young as ten and I had no idea what was happening to me.

I wasn't aware of what was to come.

It never sat well with me when things didn't go right, even when I was as young as that. During a game of football, I would let my mistakes get to me. This would lead to anger and all sorts of emotions and as a result I would get 'the breathing thing'. As I got more familiar with 'the breathing thing', I didn't let it stop me from playing. I just knew I needed to calm myself down a little bit and then carry on with the game. I used to fight the feeling. As I got older the issue obviously developed into more than just 'the breathing thing' and then it mattered a lot more, as it would hinder me at important times, but I will go into that later.

Cosham Blues wasn't the only team I was involved with growing up. I found myself playing for Portsmouth Ladies, AFC Portsmouth and I eventually got asked to go and play for Hampshire Centre of Excellence. I was with Hampshire for about five seasons from the age of 12. This was when even greater opportunities started to come, such as England Talent Camps and so on.

Fast forward, and I eventually signed for Chelsea in 2011, for the 2011/12 season with the U16s. We trained two evenings a week at the men's training facility, Cobham Training Ground, which was amazing. Being 15 years old, and the sporting maniacs that we were as kids, meant that this was not the only commitment that I and the other girls in that squad had. Many of us would also be playing for other teams such as our county or school teams.

It was nearly the end of the season and I had made it to the FA Youth Cup Final with Chelsea. The team was great. Many from this team have made it to being professionals – including Rosella Ayane and Jodie Brett (later forced into retirement through injury), although some have not.

Because I was involved with more than one team, I had played in a cup final for a different team just two days before the FA Youth Cup Final. That game had gone to extra time and penalties, so I played 120 minutes of football just over 48 hours before going into this huge game against Arsenal at the MK Dons stadium. As a kid you don't think about things like that being a problem; we played some sort of sport every day whether it was at school, at after-school clubs, or representing other clubs in other competitions.

I remember my body feeling sore before that FA Youth Cup Final, and I remember doing recovery things like using a foam roller to help my muscles recover, and getting a massage from my mum, to help my body feel ready for the Sunday. The anxiety crept up on me as the game got closer.

It was so cool being able to say my next game at the weekend was going to be the FA Cup Final. It was made that much of a big deal at school that my PE teachers at Cams Hill School arranged a minibus full of my friends to come and support my team that day. There was blue face paint and all sorts going on; it was amazing having the support I did from my friends.

It was a beautiful day and as we travelled up to Milton Keynes to meet the rest of the team, I can remember singing my heart out in the car, while every now and then getting that heart-dropping nervous feeling about the game. I don't know how my parents put up with the constant singing and screaming that happened on a regular basis to and from training and games; maybe they secretly enjoyed the racket: the joy, love and excitement they could see in my face when I was on the way to football.

The day couldn't have been any more perfect; the vibe with the girls was buzzing as always. Everyone was so excited to play, the coaches were in such good spirits. What a day this could be to remember – but unfortunately for me, although it started as a day full of nothing but joy, it soon took a turn for the worse.

In the second half I went to intercept a pass (there was no one around me) and the leg that I landed on hyperextended. I felt a kind of crack or pop in my knee and I'm sure I heard it too. I instantly went down to the ground and screamed the whole stadium down. Picture a practically empty stadium which usually holds 30,000 people, echoing with my distress. The entire place fell silent. After screaming and crying on the floor, adrenaline must have kicked in as I attempted to get up. The small crowd started clapping but as soon as I put my foot down it just felt as though my knee would just collapse. The pain was horrible. Obviously, something I had never felt before. I was scared, I was worried, what could it have been?

I got taken into the changing rooms where my physio did some tests, I had no idea what was going on to be honest, I was so young and clueless. All I cared about was watching my team. All I wanted was for us to win. I was due to go to the hospital, but I refused to go until after the game because I needed to watch my team.

The game eventually went to penalties and we won! The Arsenal team we played against had many talented footballers that made it as pros, including England's Euros-winning captain Leah Williamson, Jade Bailey, Molly Bartrip and Carla Humphreys.

Now began the process of finding out what I had done to my knee. I was 15, we didn't have any special medical backing through Chelsea at that age, so first of all I went to the hospital after the game, and I was told I had damaged my medial collateral ligament. I was given some crutches to use for a while and I then had a doctor's appointment and their conclusion was that I would be back playing in three weeks.

We weren't sure that this was correct, and the NHS waiting lists for further appointments were long, so we decided to go private. My family paid for me to get an MRI scan which showed that I had torn my anterior cruciate ligament (ACL). I remember sitting in the room and being told that news and feeling numb. I didn't really know what to think of it, I was so young. I tried not to cry, but I'm not sure I understood at that age what this meant. I had no idea what to expect.

I could sense that my dad was almost angered by the result when we got back in the car.

Looking back on it now, my dad says: 'I remember thinking that this could be the end of her career, as this type of injury had curtailed or restricted the careers of many male professional players over the years. Fortunately, this was not the case although it would be the best part of a year before she was able to play again.'

The cost of having private surgery on an ACL tear would be high, depending on the surgeon. I had a friend, Atlanta Primus, and her dad Linvoy Primus was an ex-pro footballer for Portsmouth, and he managed to help us get in contact with the surgeon who had sorted his injuries. This saved my parents about £7,000. Niall Flynn, the surgeon, spoke to us on the phone and managed to squeeze me in for a spot only two weeks after the conversation with him.

ACL ruptures must be one of the most feared injuries to have in any sport, not just football. The general process of returning to play takes about nine months. This can of course be quicker (with more risk) or slower if there are any complications or problems, it all depends on the rehabilitation. I was 16 when I had my first ACL reconstruction. This was the first time I remember seeing some sort of perspective in life. I think stepping into the unknown at any point can be scary for people but when you are so emotionally invested in something it can go one way or the other when you hit a crisis point, and luckily for me I was able to start to understand there's more to life than football. This kind of issue is something I still get caught up in and forget when things aren't going so well. Dealing with this injury was a huge turning point for me. I had so many thoughts and emotions and this moment transformed that for me in an instant.

After I had my surgery, I was unable to walk without crutches at first, but during that time the Olympic torch was going through Portsmouth so there was a huge event going on. There was live music, food, drinks all going on, on Southsea Common, which is right next to the beach. We decided to go for a family day out, but I was to go in a wheelchair to make it more comfortable for me. I was happy to be able to go and get out of the house and enjoy the experience because it hadn't been easy since the operation.

However, the joyous family day that I had hoped for soon turned out to be different. I can remember feeling so emotional and feeling like people were staring at me because I was in a wheelchair; I felt paranoid and angry.

When we got to the Common, there were thousands of people dancing and drinking and listening to the music. I was being wheeled along and I looked up and found myself catching the eye of a girl who was also in a wheelchair. My whole world stopped for a second – it was like everything around me had paused and my focus and attention turned to this girl who was looking at me as if to say, 'I know how you feel and it's okay.' It was like some sort of weird connection or understanding that I could feel without even speaking to her. Because we were both in wheelchairs, there was almost a look of relief in her face to see that someone else was in the same position as her. Little did she know that this was just a quick fix for me to get out of the house following surgery, but I felt a moment between us, and it really got to me. That was her life, and I felt as though she was happy to have seen someone who felt like she did, just for one moment. We just smiled at each other for just a few seconds, but it felt like time had just stopped. I could feel myself feeling sorry for her, feeling grateful for my life and it shook me for the rest of the day.

My family found a space in the middle of the crowd so we could enjoy the music, but I couldn't see a thing. I was so restricted, and I wasn't used to that. A man standing near us could see that I was stressed, and he leant down and pointed over to the disabled section where you could go up on your wheelchair so you could see the stage. My heart dropped when he suggested that option to us and I found it hard to hold in the tears. I just wanted to go home.

This day put so much into perspective for me, as I had only just turned 16 years old. I was going through a very challenging time in my life at a young age, having knee surgery and missing out on everything I knew. I was in a wheelchair for one day and the emotional roller coaster I experienced during it just made me realise a lot. This was only going to last a short amount of time for me, soon I would be walking and running again and eventually playing football, but the girl I saw that day could well still be in a wheelchair and that is her life. I felt lucky and it made me appreciate everything I had.

Through all those weeks and months, my parents were worrying about the negative effects the injury could have on me.

My dad says: 'The timing of all of this was also unfortunate since Millie was due to sit her GCSE exams over the coming weeks. She actually did really well in achieving a good set of results, enabling her to go on to commence her A-level studies at Itchen College. But it was sad to see Millie having to endure all of this misfortune. She had lived for sport for years and was now prevented from doing pretty much anything. She was starting college that September with her main subject being PE, and of course for the initial year this was badly impeded.'

Chapter Two

Highs and Lows at Bristol City

I WAS sat down with my family for dinner one night when I got a call from the general manager at Chelsea, Paul Green, informing me they were going to offer me a contract for the next season and would potentially be sending me on loan. What a surreal feeling that was. I was finally going to begin my professional journey; I was so ready to throw myself into it. That was a very proud day for me and my family – but the following year didn't turn out to be as perfect as I had hoped.

During my career so far, I have experienced the feeling of being stuck quite a few times. Being injured is a lonely journey. Many players don't understand how it feels to recover from a very long-term injury, although the ones that have experienced this can appreciate the mental battle one may have to go through to eventually return to the game stronger.

I have been through times in my career when I struggled with feeling like I was just having to deal with one issue after another. One of these periods ran from 2016 to 2017, when

I was on loan at Bristol City from Chelsea and was playing on a professional contract for the first time, at the age of 19. What an amazing opportunity, to go and play for a different club in the league below, to get game time and improve my skills. Unfortunately, this was the beginning of a run of bad luck for me.

Being at Bristol on loan was an extremely exciting time. I turned pro and had gone away with every intention of proving what I could do, to get better, and learn. Being with a team that all had the same goal and ambition – promotion to WSL 1 (Women's Super League 1, the top tier of the women's game) – made it even more exciting. I made new friends, some that I would class as friends for life, and was having such a good time playing football full-time and living away from home.

I moved in with some team-mates to a house on a road called Wood Street. Wow, there are some crazy memories and stories from living in that house. We would have so much fun over the most pathetic things, I guess that showed our age. From pet chickens to police knocking on our door because of shining laser pens through people's windows, lighting fires in the garden which exploded, honestly the list goes on, the stories could probably have their own books there are so many. As time went on, we all started to bond and create a really positive team environment.

As the season started, we knew how important it was to get points from every game with promotion to WSL 1 being our goal. We all believed in the plan and wanted it badly. It was a completely new environment for me, coming from Chelsea, where I was unsure where I stood. I loved being at Bristol. I had visions of being the top goalscorer in the league and of going on to bigger things – you know, a typical vision of a 19-year-old starting their professional career. Of course, any career comes with external and internal doubts, in fact any walk of life does really, when you think about it, but when you want something, you keep pushing regardless.

The season began and it was amazing. I felt valued, and I was absolutely buzzing for every game. But this feeling didn't last too long, as in our second WSL 2 match, the first little blip happened. All I wanted was to be able to play football and enjoy the experience, but it seemed that wasn't going to happen.

We were playing Sheffield, and this was a big game because they were a decent side, and it meant a lot for me to do well because I had friends and family coming to watch me kick off my professional career. I have often wondered whether or not subconsciously I put more pressure on myself to do well when there are people I really care about watching. Did this mean I tried too hard on this occasion, which resulted in an outcome I didn't want?

It was an evening game and us footballers always say we love to play under the lights; it just feels like a special occasion for some reason and it's true there is a different feeling about it – although I didn't like waiting around all day for kick-off because that gave more time for nerves to kick in.

I can picture myself turning up with that excitement for the game to come, having the best time with my team, dancing in the changing rooms before the warm-up.

Anyway, towards the end of the game, if I remember rightly, I went to use my arm to shield someone while trying to win the ball (it's kind of a blur) and this resulted in my shoulder dislocating. I went straight into a state of shock and was screaming very loudly every swear word under the sun. I have had a lot of people joke with me about that, but it was offensive, to be fair. My dad still moans at me for swearing too much now!

My first thought was that I had broken my arm, but I was certain there was something not right. My shoulder was out of its socket and the pain was actually vile.

After I had calmed down a little, the physio and doctor helped me off the pitch and into the changing rooms so they could attempt to get the shoulder back in place. I was on gas and air to try and ease the pain, as I was still screaming at this point. Mum and Dad had made it into the changing room area, and my sister Eden as well, but my dad wasn't allowed to go in as the game had nearly finished so the team would soon be back in the changing room.

I was laying on the bed sucking in as much of the gas and air as I could. The doctor had assessed the shoulder and confirmed it was out of its socket, so he then explained to me (although I can't really recall it), my mum and sister what he was about to do in order to relocate it. I agreed for him to do it, as I didn't want to wait until I went to the hospital; I was in so much pain I just needed it to go back in. All I can remember is the effects of the gas and air and me screaming the changing room down as he proceeded to put it back in its socket.

Eden has a much clearer memory of it all than I do, as she explains here:

'It was the first time I had been to one of Millie's games in a little while. It was an evening game meaning the whole pitch was lit with floodlights and I remember feeling a slight sense of anticipation throughout the game; I always do when I watch Millie play.

'Whenever Millie goes down in a game there's always a few seconds afterwards where I try to figure out if she's okay or not. I think this is something I've always done, even before the first ACL injury. On this particular occasion I remember realising quickly that this was going to be one of the bad ones.

'I remember looking at my parents and seeing their panic and them quickly leaving the stand to run towards the changing rooms. I was left in the stand with one of Millie's friends. Straight away I didn't feel right being sat there not knowing what was going on. I was a lot younger at the time so I didn't really know if I was even allowed to see Millie. I guess little protective sister mode kicked in and not long after my parents left, I took off towards the changing rooms.

'I don't remember specifically how I got there but I made my way into the girls' changing room where I saw Millie laying on a table/stretcher in the centre of the room. She was clearly in shock and a lot of pain. It was always quite distressing seeing her in these states but I knew that was where I was meant to be.

'A very helpful and calm doctor came into the changing room and gave Millie some gas and air which seemed to help with the pain. He then went on to ask if she would rather wait and go to hospital to get the shoulder put back in or if she felt comfortable having it placed back there and then. Millie quickly said to "put it in now" through pained breaths. He explained what this would consist of: "I'm going to pull your arm down and push it back up into position," I think is vaguely what he said.

'After a countdown from three, I looked away, Millie let out a huge scream and quickly it was over. She then had help getting changed out of her kit and her arm was tied in a sling. At some point the game finished and the rest of the girls came into the changing rooms. All of them gave her little pats and hugs before we left.

'That's pretty much everything I remember from the night. My memories of these occasions tend to be a little blurred by the adrenaline response from watching something bad happen to someone you love. I remember thinking she's some kind of super-human though, telling the doctor to fix it there and then. Nutter.'

As soon as it went back in, it was like this crazy relief from the pain, but then comes the aftermath of such an incident. The doctor advised me to go to the hospital for an X-ray in case there was any bone that may have chipped off, that could cause further discomfort. So, I decided to go back to a hospital near my parents' home (rather than in Bristol) and I went in the car with some of my friends that had come to watch the game.

I was gutted, all the visions, plans and expectations in my head had started to fall apart. The frustration wasn't only from me but from my family as well. My dad was clearly affected by what happened and when I got home, we had a very heated row which consisted of him trying to tell me how I could have avoided such a thing happening, while my enraged response did not go down too well and I ended up just leaving the house with my friend who was taking me to hospital. I almost had a feeling of letting him down. This has happened at various times in my career, but I will go on to that later. On reflection, it is all about perception.

The scan came back and there was no sign of any chipped bone so I was free to go back to Chelsea to proceed with my rehabilitation.

I would not be where I am today without the support I have from my mum and dad. They really have been through it all with me. The highest of highs and the lowest of lows.

They have celebrated all of the wins, goals and positive times and also been there to pick me up when I have been on the floor ready to give up. When it comes to football though, it has always been a little bit different with Dad. I think it is very natural for parents to be quite involved in the emotion of the game. After all, they were the ones that would drive for hours on end through the week and on the weekend to make sure I was at training and games when I was younger. The sacrifices they made for me to be able to get to this level are something I will always be thankful for. There have been many disagreements, arguments, and heated discussions regarding football between me and Dad. I know deep down it is only because he cares, and he wants me to do well and achieve what he feels I deserve. I am aware that supportive parents are something not everyone has. But when it comes to my career, it almost feels like everything that is happening to me, happens to him too. Hence the reaction he had when my shoulder came out. Upon reflection I do believe it is because he never used to deal with it very well when things did not go to plan, or when he had an expectation of what should have happened in his eyes, and it didn't.

I think I did put pressure on myself for this reason, as I know he is a proud parent and is proud of the fact that I am living my dream, so he would tell all his clients about me and keep them updated on my journey. This obviously started to create feelings within me that I never wanted to let my parents down. You will read more about this in the Second Half of this book.

I had to return to Chelsea for rehab and recovery. During this period it was made clear to me that there was a chance that the shoulder could come out again, even after strengthening it through the rehab, and if it did, surgery would be required. I continued to work hard, determined as ever, and once I got the all-clear I went back to training with Bristol.

This takes us to a match against Durham away. I felt like I was having a good game and I was enjoying myself. But in the second half I went to challenge for a ball and a girl grabbed my arm and pulled on it hard. There it was – the re-dislocation of the same shoulder. In that moment when it came out, it hit me that my season would probably be over, and I was going to have to undergo the surgery. Those thoughts made it so hard for me to stay calm. I came off the pitch and was taken straight into the changing rooms. Straight on the gas and air (this seemed to be my new best mate). The physios and doctors tried to put my shoulder back in but it just wouldn't happen. They tried everything, pulling it, twisting it at every angle but it would not budge. I will let your imagination take you down that path. You should have seen my face when my physio suggested that the next option was for me to try and put it back in myself. Chris explained how I was to try and do it by laying on my front and doing the action of raising my arm to take a drink. I looked at him distraught, like 'no mate, fuck that'. I couldn't think of anything worse; I felt sick I was in that much pain, and I did not have it in me to put my own shoulder back in its socket.

A few of the girls came in to see me when the whistle had blown. I was completely out of it on gas and air, but I remember my mate Jodie singing songs to me through a stethoscope and using other pieces of medical equipment to try and make me laugh. The medics had called an ambulance, but this sort of incident isn't seen as a priority and the wait was to be around four hours to get me to hospital and get my shoulder back in.

Since the ambulance was going to be a long time and we were supposed to be going back to Bristol as a team on the bus, the doctor offered to drive us to the hospital he worked at. Every movement was agony: imagine your shoulder being in completely the wrong place just hanging there. I managed to get in the back of his car and my physio Chris sat next to me, holding my arm and shoulder in a comfortable position for the full duration of the journey. About halfway there the gas and air ran out and I was fuming. All I remember is being out of it and seeing the Angel of the North out of the window, wondering what the hell was going on. We made it to hospital and my team decided they would wait for me. Our staff and manager took them all to get pizza while I had my shoulder put back in. I was given a local anaesthetic and I pretty much passed out. They put a sheet under my arm pit, pulled on that while someone else pulled on my arm and eventually it went back in. After that, we then started the long journey back to Bristol on the bus. I was not in a good way. I felt so sick, and I remember I couldn't eat anything and when I tried, I threw it back up. The poor girls had to listen to me retching a lot of the way home. What a lovely journey that must have been for them.

Every time a player gets injured, we spend time away from the football pitch and when we return, we have lost some of our sharpness, mentally and physically. I have always wanted to get to the top, to play at the top level. But in the early years of my career my luck with injuries and the effect it was having on me mentally was stopping me from getting anywhere near.

I had to have an operation on the shoulder this time, to try to stop it from dislocating again in the future.

My surgeon was Andrew Wallace, who had performed the same surgery on athletes such as rugby players and it had something like a 99 per cent success rate regarding re-dislocation, so it was fair to say I trusted him fully. Basically, the surgery consisted of getting anchors put into my shoulder to help prevent it dislocating again.

I turned up for the procedure and I was in good spirits, messing around in the hospital. I got given paper pants that I had to change into, and even though I was about to go through another surgery I wasn't taking myself too seriously, dancing around the hospital room in my gown and paper pants. I stood on the windowsill and started singing 'God

Save the Queen'. The staff at the hospital must have thought, 'what a weirdo'.

I woke up from the surgery and I remember not being able to feel my whole left arm, the entire thing was numb. It was a very strange feeling which lasted about a day. I had to use my other hand to move my left hand as it felt so uncomfortable.

Chelsea as a club were brilliant with me medically but I never really felt part of the team in the same way I did at Bristol. There was just a different energy about it.

So, following my surgery, I really wanted to return to Bristol for the last two games of the season, which happened to be the most important, as we were so close to our goal of getting promotion. I remember telling the physios that I wanted to be ready for Everton away, which was the second to last game of the season, as a win would secure us promotion. I managed to make it back for the game and I scored as well, helping my team win 3-2. The game had everything: two teams battling till the end with the same vision of the league above. We even had a pitch invader and that does not happen often in the women's game. Injury time stretched to about eight minutes, which was unbelievable. I remember getting subbed off and none of us were sitting on the bench; we were all just screaming at the referee to blow the whistle. During injury time, Everton had a penalty which was saved.

The scenes were immense. We did it! We secured promotion and we were heading to the top league with this amazing group of girls. These are the moments that make all the hard work and suffering worthwhile.

Despite the season being very up and down for me I still managed to be the top goalscorer at Bristol City that season and the second-top goalscorer in the league, which was a special achievement for me considering the injuries. I had gained a lot of experience on and off the pitch and really started to learn about myself as a person at this point. It confirmed to me that this was exactly what I wanted to do but also that it wasn't going to be an easy ride.

Chapter Three

Forced to Respond to a New Struggle

BEING EXPOSED to experiences that we aren't comfortable with is how we grow and develop as people. In many cases these experiences are ones that we haven't chosen and are unplanned. As a footballer the place I want to be is on the football pitch. When we learn to accept that this isn't always going to be the case because of the high risk of injury in playing, it is also a time when we can allow ourselves to grow in ways that we may not be able to see.

Everyone experiences trauma, disappointment, failure and loss. We are not defined by these challenges; we are defined by the way we respond and react to them.

If we respond to the struggle in the right way then we will not just be better off, but we will be better off more quickly. This is something that has taken me a while to learn, and I am still working on today.

It was April 2017. I had been on an England camp all week. I can remember driving back with my friend Ellie

Wilson, singing our hearts out on the way back to Bristol. We were scheduled to have a friendly the next day, against a team of boys and men from Bristol, as it was two weeks until the Spring Series started, which I was so excited about because we would be playing our first game at Ashton Gate (Bristol City's men's ground).

After dislocating my shoulder twice in 2016, I was so determined to come back and have an injury-free season and prove myself. This will be the year, I kept telling myself.

Matchday was the day of the Grand National. Kick-off wasn't until later in the day so me and some of the girls spent the day chilling, putting bets on the horses and catching up really.

I can remember saying to one of the girls that there wasn't much point in us playing in the friendly because we were so tired from camp, and it was against a random team, not one linked to the academy or anything. I always used to be very sceptical about playing against boys, due to the physical differences between genders. They are so much stronger physically, so in any kind of contact the female is probably going to be worse off.

I said to one of the girls, 'If I get injured in this game, I'll be fuming.'

Anyhow, I wasn't starting the game, which I was glad about because of the way I was feeling after the week. I can also remember feeling my ankle a little bit from a recent ankle roll, but other than that I was happy, enjoying myself, the weather was amazing and I couldn't wait to see if I had won any money on the horses.

We were into the second half and my manager Willie Kirk turned to me and asked if I wanted to go on. Looking back now, I wish I had not said yes. But of course, I was going to say yes. I am a footballer, I want to play football and, in that moment, no matter how tired I was, I was always going to say yes. Even if it was a meaningless friendly.

I got subbed on and about ten minutes into my time the ball was played to me. Nobody was around me, except a defender in front of me who I wanted to beat, so I went to drop my shoulder to try and show him one way, but when I planted my foot I had an instant pain through my knee, almost like an in-shock feeling. I went down straight away but didn't scream or anything like that, I just held my knee.

The physio came on and I hobbled off. He said, 'We will have a look and you can go back on,' but I said, 'I can't go back on.' So, he strapped it up with ice and I sat and watched the remainder of the game with a face on. I was probably sat there thinking 'why me, why is it always me who gets some sort of injury?', even though at this point I had no idea what was wrong with it, but I didn't think it was bad at all. The physio assessed me inside after the game and I was functional and still had strength, the only thing I couldn't do was straighten my leg. I just thought I had tweaked something, and it would be fine in two weeks, just in time for the Spring Series. My mate Ellie Wilson had to drive my car back because I couldn't.

I started to convince myself that it was fine, and I would be fine. I couldn't even bear the thought of telling my dad I thought I was injured again because I knew he would be so upset. Every time I got any sort of injury, I dreaded telling my parents because they care so much and want me to do well. They feel the pain of the heartbreak that their daughter is feeling just like any parent would for their child. It is not just me that is injured, it is them too.

I spoke with my parents that day and I didn't mention anything on the phone. I didn't want them to worry or think my chances of doing well were going to be affected. But that soon changed when the Bristol physio wanted me to come in to see him on one of the days after the game. I went in and he did his checks, and he went on to say I should go back to Chelsea to have a scan because he thought it could be something to do with my ACL.

I don't know if it was the term 'ACL' that made me feel like this, but I was furious inside; I was quite rude. I actually think I laughed in his face and said, 'It's not my ACL.' I was thinking, 'You don't know what you're talking about,' and I said, 'Can't we wait to see if it settles down first and then scan if it hasn't?' I genuinely didn't think a scan was necessary. I don't know whether it was because I had done my other ACL before and they just didn't compare in terms of the feeling and the pain when it happened.

Anyway, the fact that he wanted me to go back to Chelsea for a scan then made me panic. I was straight on the phone to my girlfriend at the time crying my eyes out on the 3G pitch where we trained, next to the physio room, telling her, 'He doesn't know what he's on about.' I think I was saying 'what if this, what if that'. I was Googling how my knee felt to try and get to some sort of conclusion about what it could be. I was trying to self-diagnose, which we all know never ends well. Anyway, I was in such a state because I let my mind take over, the thoughts turned into emotion and the feeling of anger. I had to call my mum to finally tell her what was going on. I rang her and made her promise not to tell my dad anything because there was still a bit of hope that it could have been nothing or could have been minor.

Soon afterwards, I found myself on my way to Cobham to get assessed by the Chelsea physios. My girlfriend drove me because I still couldn't drive. Two of my other team-mates came too. The drive was about an hour and a half to get there, maybe longer; I was nervous and anxious, but I wasn't too bad. The others dropped me off and they all went into Cobham while I went in to see the physio.

It was always nice to go back to the training ground to see people I hadn't seen in a while but that was the last thing on my mind at this moment; I just wanted to know what I had done. I got assessed by a physio and then later had to go up to the men's first-team building, which was always a nerve-racking experience because they were the big dogs. I had to wait outside while our physio went in, until I was called in. There must have been about seven different physios and doctors in the room. I had to go in and get on the bed and let various people come and have a look at the knee. They did all kinds of tests on it, and I had to perform different exercises so they could see whether I could do them. Anyway, when they were finished, I then had to leave the room again while they discussed what was going to happen next. Apparently in that chat they nearly said a scan wasn't necessary but my physio had explained about my injury history and the outcome was that I was to go for a scan later that day.

I got given a time and a place and was expected to be there. This is when the horrible feelings and thoughts would start to take over. I was going to find out in a couple of hours what I had done. All I could think about was how my world was about to potentially change massively. How am I going to tell my parents? I'm going to have to leave Bristol and move back home, away from my team, my girlfriend, the place I now classed as my home. What is the extent of the injury? How long will I be out for? All these questions ran through my head uncontrollably, as I was thinking about the fact that in a few hours my whole life would be completely different after this result.

I went for the scan, and we made our way back to the training ground to find out the result. I got called in to the doctor's room and I sat down with Dr Paco Biosca. He is

Spanish and sometimes I didn't really understand what he said. I thought he said, 'It's good news,' so my face brightened up and I replied 'Good news?' But then he carried on, 'No, no, it is not good news.' My whole world came crumbling down as he went on to say I had torn my ACL. From that moment I was numb. I knew what was coming, I knew what process I was about to go through, and I tried to hold in my tears, but I couldn't. The nightmare that could've been, was happening. He said some other things that I can't remember, because as soon as I heard it was my ACL I just switched off. I was heartbroken, the footballer's worst nightmare was about to happen to me for the second time. I left the room, and my physio went on to sort of comfort me but also gave me a load of information regarding the surgery and other things I cannot remember. I just remember looking at him in a broken way and tried to hold in my emotions and tears.

I went out to the car, got in and broke down uncontrollably, that kind of ugly crying where your nose is running and you are kind of shouting everything you're saying. I called my mum to tell her the result, I was in hysterics because I care so much about making them proud and getting somewhere in this fucking sport. At this point she obviously needed to tell my dad. I actually think I may have said sorry for what was going on. I cared so much.

I later learned that my mum had already filled my dad in on what was going on and he was already a little bit prepared for the result. It was a big blur to be honest. He sent me this text not long after as I couldn't really speak on the phone properly in that state:

'It was a cruel twist and totally undeserved. Another mountain to climb, but one day the view from the top will be worth all this shit.'

I got home from the long journey back to Bristol and none of the girls were in the house. I didn't know what to do with myself, I felt like I went into some robotic state or something and I just remember starting to pack all of my stuff up.

It was now time to try and let it sink in, try and mentally prepare myself for the physical and mental challenge ahead. Time to try and accept it – and that is something that used to take a long time for me.

Surgery took place on 19 April 2017. Me and Dad were put up in a hotel not far from the Bupa Cromwell Hospital in London and all I can remember was feeling so nervous and anxious about the surgery, whether it was going to be a success, etc. We went to a little Italian place down the road from the hotel to get some dinner which was a struggle; even the fact that I knew I wasn't going to be allowed to eat anything in the time leading up to the surgery wasn't making me feel hungry.

I didn't get much sleep that night and it was an early rise to head down to the hospital for us. When you get sent to your room you just have to wait, wait until it is your turn to go under the knife. I think there was some cricket on TV and this guy kept hitting six after six which was enough to keep me distracted for a few minutes before getting that heart-dropping feeling. It's a strange thing, you feel okay, you're distracted and then the slightest thing will remind you of everything you're scared of or worried about. This circle of feeling kept going until I was put to sleep.

I was collected from my room in the bed and wheeled down to surgery. The anaesthetist was trying to make me feel comfortable, making jokes about what alcohol I like drinking and saying that I was about to feel drunk, then he counted down and I blacked out. I knew that when I woke up it would be the start: the start of the pain, the start of the suffering but also the start of a new adventure.

One of the strangest things is waking up in recovery. The morphine hits straight away and you start chatting shit to the doctor or nurse that is looking after you. Falling in and out of sleep, you await the time you get given the go-ahead to go back to your room.

I had plans for some of my friends to come and visit me, as I had to stay the night in the hospital, so they drove all the way from Bristol to London to see me for a few hours. They left straight after training, and all turned up in their Bristol kit. Obviously even after major surgery I was still trying to provide the entertainment, with the help of morphine of course. It was lucky I had my own room or I probably would have been heavily judged for some of the things that I was shouting. I got given a cuddly toy pig and there's a video of me with it in my arms and I say 'Oh piggy, I knew one day we'd be together.' I have no idea what the meaning was behind that, but again, morphine. I was being well looked after as it was a private hospital, the food was being served in silver cloches, but I wasn't interested in anything other than Domino's pizza. I'm pretty sure I got what I wanted and smashed a few slices.

Although I had been through this surgery before, it was significantly different from the first time. I don't remember it being that painful the first time. I was expected to be in for rehab a day after the surgery had taken place, but I was in no state to be going. I was in so much pain, and I now realise that it was not only physical but mental.

During my recovery I thought it would be a good idea to write down how I felt in a diary. I didn't know or plan how much I was going to write or even when I was going to write. I just did sometimes, when I felt like it. At the start I was just sitting down all the time, basically disabled for a while, as you know from the first ACL injury back in 2012. So, it gave me something to do for a bit.

Looking back at some of the things I wrote makes me laugh a little, maybe because things are completely different now, but the reality of it is, I really did feel that way and how we feel is so important. Feelings shouldn't be fought or ignored. Feelings should be felt and dealt with in the right way.

Here are some extracts from my diary during that recovery period.

Friday 21 April

It's been two days since my surgery and I don't think I could feel any worse. The pain is terrible and it's so hard not to feel sorry for myself, especially seeing everyone on social media posting about the first game of the Spring Series, which takes place tomorrow. It's at Ashton Gate, which is such a special occasion for the club, one that I was very much looking forward to. The fact I won't be playing a part is absolutely killing me. One of the hardest parts is knowing that it is going to be like this for the next six to nine months. Not only will I not be part of it, but I am going to be spending most of my days at Chelsea for rehab. It feels like Bristol and the girls there have been snatched away from me. It's devastating how something can happen in your life and make you feel like you have been left with nothing. Nothing that people say can make me feel better at this stage.

Although it feels like I am miles and miles away from where I want to be, I know that I will get there eventually. Right now, I feel so alone. I want to go to the game but in this state of pain, it doesn't seem sensible and I don't know if I am ready to face it.

Game day – Saturday 22 April

I was really gutted that I couldn't go to the game but even though I wasn't there, the girls made me feel like I was. Every player wore a warm-up top which had 'Farrow 9' printed on the back. It was so amazing to see, and know that I have the support of my whole team. It was a really special touch and I appreciated it so much.

The messages I received from my team-mates since finding out I have done my ACL have been amazing as well. Sometimes words won't make a difference to how you feel, but sometimes they can lift you up to where you want to be.

Sometimes (when I wasn't injured) I wondered what my team-mates thought of my footballing ability. I often thought it. I think it must be something to do with my OCD. But reading some of the messages that got sent really lifted my confidence. It is important that I stay positive through this process (even if that is easy to say). So, I think reminding myself of things people have said or say to me will really help at times.

Here are a couple of the messages from my team-mates that particularly meant a lot in that moment:

'You don't deserve that not one bit, but you know what, I've seen how hard you work for every inch and every millimetre – you will come back through this stronger physically and mentally. You've established yourself on the pitch and people are going to chew your arm off to get you once you're back recovering so don't worry about that.'

'You've been so unlucky in the last year. But once you're back from this setback, you will be flying. Injury-free and on to building an immense career in football. You're such a talented footballer and an absolutely amazing girl who lights up any room. And someone who has brought so much in such a short space at Bristol.'

Tuesday 25 April – first day of rehab

The rush of emotions I have felt today would be enough to mentally drain anyone. I got out of the car and started to make my way over to the physio room and at this point I already had tears in my eyes. I already felt my emotions were running high and when I spoke I had to try really hard not to let myself tear up.

Rehab began and I felt like it was going relatively well. The part I was hating most was extensions. Toby had to force my knee into extension and the pain was disgusting. Honestly vile.

After lunch we did similar to what we did in the morning but Toby left at 3 so Aaron did my extension work. I felt sick, it hurt that much. I cried because it felt so sore. Biting my jumper really hard while thinking about not wanting to do this anymore.

I couldn't wait to get home. I was there about 11.30am and I didn't leave until 5. I got into the car and burst into tears. What I just experienced is absolutely horrible and the thing that makes it worse is knowing I will have to go through it again tomorrow.

I was shattered, which didn't help my emotions. When I got home, I cried desperately to my mum.

I got on with the Game Ready – a machine that ices and compresses your knee. I had to keep a straight leg. I don't think I can even put in writing how uncomfortable and painful that was. I was crying and screaming helplessly.

'If I ever do my ACL again then I will never play football again,' are some of the words that came out of my mouth afterwards. This is Day One! I have struggled so much today. I have been miserable with my family, pretty shit with my girlfriend, but the way I feel is unique. It is not a nice feeling at all and nobody can do anything to make me feel better.

I hate seeing people so happy on their social media when I am here feeling like this. Alone. I can't be that person though: that person who is angry, jealous and upset at seeing others being all happy.

Day One has been a horrible hurdle that, yes, I got over, but the hurdles that remain become taller and stronger. The next six to nine months will be hell most of the time but I need to be able to reach heaven. So whatever hurdle I need to cross, I need to make sure I fucking cross it.

Tuesday 2 May

My knee actually felt quite good today which is obviously a positive. It is hard because I keep thinking too far ahead, when I need to be taking each day as it comes. In this situation you certainly get a lot of time to think/over-think. Sometimes positively, sometimes negatively. A lot of negative thoughts tend to come more than positive at this stage. Part of me still can't believe this is happening but it is reality and I am living it. My life is almost on hold right now while I climb this mountain.

Reading these diary entries now makes me feel many different things. It really does take me back to that feeling of sadness and struggle. I can see the emotions I was feeling at the time from reading the diary, I can see how I was processing the situations; it is so interesting for me to read. I can see how much I was hurting mentally but I was so determined to come back from it. It is refreshing as well, because I am noticing how I was almost talking myself through the situation. It's a sort of therapy and you can see that it was working. I was helping myself realise things by writing them down and I can see my mindset changing throughout the process.

I almost feel embarrassed knowing that I felt that way, knowing how sorry I felt for myself. It does show how deeply I cared about the situation I was in. It shows how emotionally attached I was and still am to the game; to proving myself and achieving. Which is why it is so important that I wrote down how I felt. It shows how far I have come; it proves I can improve my mindset and overcome things I never thought I could.

I don't care for the judging that came with this process; I already judged myself enough, so I don't care what other people think of me now. It is reality, the feelings and thoughts I experienced are real life. It is so eye-opening for me to read this back and it made me giggle a bit. If only I could have put things into perspective then as well as I can today, the tough days may not have been so bad.

Thursday 18 May

Last night I came up to Bristol to surprise the girls for when they got back from their game. I got in the house and waited for the girls to come in. I shouted at the top of my voice 'When I say wood, you say street' (it was this stupid chant we used to do) and everyone sprinted upstairs. It sounded like a stampede. My legs were actually shaking as I was so excited and emotional to see them. I felt so happy, I hadn't seen them in ages and I was going through this shit and had felt like I was alone. It was so good to spend time in Bristol even if it was only for a day and a night. I am calling it a 'reset'.

I had a catch-up with Willie [Kirk, the manager] today which was really good. We spoke about a lot of things but the main thing I took away from it was some news he told me. When I found out I had done my ACL, in a text Willie told me he was talking about me at the England game, and it was all positive. He never actually told me what was said until today. He said he couldn't tell me because he didn't feel like it was a good time as I had just had the bad news about my injury. He basically told me that the England goalkeeper coach was watching our FA Cup game against Man City and was really impressed with me, and the current England manager Mark Sampson was talking positively about me as he had seen me play at the England camp before I did the injury. Apparently, he said something like 'that Farrow has got a bit about her'.

I was really happy to hear all of this, especially when I had spent a lot of time putting myself down and underestimating myself. It has given me confidence and I will use that as motivation. I feel reset and this will all help me get on with getting back to football.

Nothing may have even come from these comments, I guess I will never know, but knowing they were said was enough to give me the boost I needed and that bit of motivation that reminded me why I was coming back from the injury.

While I was using a diary to get some of the emotions off my chest, my parents were having to deal with seeing their daughter upset and in pain once again.

My dad says: 'For us it was a repeat of that same helpless feeling that there was nothing we could influence or change. As with all our children, we had always tried to offer support along their chosen paths and to help them make the most of their opportunities. Perhaps naively, it never occurred to us that injury could be such a dominant factor in Millie's career and development.

'Because of the way in which Millie had advanced through the youth system there was almost an expectation that this pattern of development would continue. While aware of the injury risks associated with sport, I had no inclination that injuries would play such a significant role in Millie's career, almost to the point of defining it!

'When she tore her second ACL I felt great disappointment and, to a degree, disbelief. In addition, a feeling that you really don't deserve to be dealt these cards time after time. I'm a great believer in the concept that hard work and effort should result in rewards, but in Millie's case all her determination and effort seemed to simply be undone by another significant barrier (physical or mental).'

My dad sometimes seems to dive deeply into thoughts of how other players' careers are going, compared to mine. 'It's probably a symptom of the disappointment and the perceived unfairness of it,' he says. 'One serious injury is bad enough, but when you get up to the five or six Millie has suffered it breaks your heart. Other players that have stayed fit and been backed by their managers have gone on to great things including representing their national teams. While this is great to see it is also difficult to take!

'We have always had conversations along the lines of "it could be worse, think of people in a worse situation than you", and gradually, as the return to fitness is achieved you start to think of the potential and future success. But often this has been scuppered by the next injury or problem.'

The way I see it now is that we never know truly what is going on in someone's life or head, no matter how successful they seem from the media and social media. Just because they play for a big club or earn large amounts of money, it doesn't necessarily mean they are happy. It also doesn't mean that they aren't experiencing their own struggle or personal problems. This is something I have always tried to help my dad understand when he comments on players that I have played with who now play for England seniors and are at 'big clubs' such as Man City etc. I know the injury side of it has more of an effect on him, but my story is my reality. It is so easy for him to compare me with people I have played with, to say 'what if this' and 'what if that', and 'that could have been you if this hadn't happened'. But it isn't; it isn't me and I am okay with that. All the setbacks happened to me, and I am hands down a better person because of it.

The rehab process is very intense, especially when at a club like Chelsea. I started off travelling from my home every day, and someone had to give me a lift there and back six days every week, as I wasn't allowed to drive my car for three months after the surgery. I relied heavily on my parents and it was a lot to ask: 720 miles a week to get me to and from rehab.

I was so grateful to be able to recover there. Not many clubs have the luxuries that they have. There was another girl who had done her ACL, Jade Bailey. We became close through the recovery but knew which days we wanted to talk and which days we would rather be anywhere else but there. Through the time I was rehabbing, there were four different players recovering from ACL injuries. I became close to my physio Toby, we ended up being like brother and sister. I wasn't afraid to tell him what I thought, and I liked that we had that relationship. It makes it easier when going through a mentally challenging injury. He secretly put together an amazing video of my recovery that I still have to this day. It includes messages from my friends and family and snippets of me doing different stages of rehab.

We were able to use the men's facilities at certain times of the day – either before 8am or after 4–5pm when the men's first team wouldn't be there. However, either one of these options would mean being stuck in shit traffic on the way there or back. As the process carried on, I knew I was struggling mentally but I couldn't bear the thought of showing it. I ended up having a few sessions with Tim Harkness, the Chelsea sports psychologist. I spoke with him about a lot of things, some that I will go into later. I remember telling him that I wanted to learn to play the drums. Not too long after that he arranged that Petr Cech would come down and have a chat with me and lend me his portable drum kit. He set it up and then started playing 'Yellow' by Coldplay on the drums. Cool geezer.

As rehab neared the final stages, they were a lot more lenient about when we could be in the first-team building. I ended up having good conversations with John Terry, David Luiz and lots of the first-team staff, who are brilliant. I was doing some outdoor rehab and John Terry came down and went in goal for me for a bit: of course, I scored against him! I played football tennis with David Luiz as well when he was recovering from an injury and was spending a lot of time in the gym.

Chapter Four

A Big Step Forward,
and Another Step Back

AFTER MY first season at Bristol, before my second ACL injury, I had agreed to stay there for the six-month Spring Series. When I had met Emma Hayes and Paul Green at the Chelsea training ground to discuss what was next, I was so certain I wanted to return to Bristol City to play in the Spring Series, I didn't even bat an eyelid when Emma mentioned that Reading had shown interest in me at that point. I guess I felt like I had unfinished business at Bristol and I was happy to stay, as I enjoyed the environment so much. That being said, it was obviously amazing to have interest from a Women's Super League (WSL) 1 club at the time. In hindsight maybe if I had taken that move, I wouldn't have ruptured my ACL, but I have learned not to think like that. It doesn't help. What was meant for me, happened.

So, when I started to near the end of my ACL recovery, I needed to think about where I was going to play for the second half of the season. I always had Bristol in mind because I knew they would take me back after conversations with Willie Kirk. I had been part of helping them to win promotion to WSL 1 and I just needed to be playing again after the lengthy time away from the pitch.

It was such a strange time. I almost ended up agreeing to go and play in Norway at a club called Klepp. One of the coaches at Chelsea, Rob Udberg, was almost a bit of a football 'dad' to me (years later, we are still in contact and keep up to date with each other's careers, which is nice) and he flew out with me to go and meet the manager. However, I was so mentally drained from the rehab, I didn't feel ready to go to play abroad. For that, and other reasons, the option ended up falling through, and I was on my way back to Bristol. When the decision was made to go back to Bristol, I made a mutual agreement with Chelsea to terminate my contract with them early and I signed permanently with Bristol until the end of the season.

When you come back from a big injury, it does take you a long while to feel 'normal' again. It was hard being one of the lower teams in WSL 1 – you don't get much of the ball and as a striker in that team I found myself just running and running and running – which may have contributed to the cause of a back problem which, unknown to me, was looming.

I remember playing against Arsenal, I went back for a corner and jumped up to head the ball and I got an elbow to the head. Instantly it was streaming with blood. The physio ran on the pitch to sort me out. I had blood in my eyes and all I could see was red. My thoughts were 'fuck this, I'm not coming off the pitch'. I was fucking fed up with it, one thing after another. So, I went off at the side of the pitch and I told Willie I was going to go back on. The doctor came over and stitched my head up in that moment. I held on to a couple of the girls' hands while the needle went through my head, I think four times. He wrapped my head in bandages like I was some sort of injured soldier. I changed my shirt as it was covered in blood and went back on. I wasn't going to be stopped. I walked past the crowd at half-time and saw Mum and Dad, I wanted them to see that I was okay. Dad was again very stressed.

Anyway, luckily for me, I must have done enough to keep Kelly Chambers (the Reading manager) interested as that following summer, she offered me a two-year contract at Reading. I couldn't believe it when I heard the news. It was exciting and a huge opportunity again. Summer is a tricky one for footballers when they are out of contract or trying to find a new club. It's a weird period: you're supposed to be resting and recovering, switching off from the football world, but it is always the total opposite. Entering the unknown, relying on agents and managers to get back to you. That switch-off time can easily turn into mind-overdrive time. It is understandably an anxious time for players. I was away on holiday with my family while it was all going on and I just couldn't seem to take my mind off the outcome, checking my phone for updates and sending messages asking questions constantly. I will go into this more when I talk about my learnings later in the book. Eventually, the deal went through, and I was going to be a Reading player for the next two years. I cried when my agent told me. Shock, I was an emotional wreck. Have you noticed yet? I feel my emotions very deeply. Good and bad.

This was finally the break I wanted, a chance to come to a decent club and prove myself in the Women's Super League. Not only to the people around me but to myself as well. Could all of the hard work, struggle and pain finally begin to be paying off? I couldn't wait to get started with Reading Football Club. A fresh start, new team, new location. Time to make my family proud after all the injuries and hard times I have faced for football. It all seemed too good to be true and I guess it was.

Towards the end of my time at Bristol I had begun to feel pain in my back. With the lack of resources and expertise at Bristol, it was no surprise that no one ever got to the bottom of what it was, but at the time I was still able to train and play, I was just in a lot of pain. So, before games I was taking painkillers as strong as co-codamol so that I wasn't thinking about it during the game. Anyway, the season came to an end, and I had time off but with the potential of signing for Reading I wanted to make sure I was in reasonable shape when I arrived there for pre-season. Still not knowing what could be wrong with my back I carried on as normal, going to the gym to complete my programme and going out running, still being in pain.

I wasn't convinced that it would be anything serious, so I tried to keep up with all the training. Eventually I was having to take strong painkillers before completing any exercise. I would be running on the treadmill and feeling this horrible sharp pinching pain in my lower back. I would stop running, try to stretch out the muscles around it which made it feel better for a short while, but the cycle would continue.

Eventually I reached out to a private physio, who I had seen after my first ACL injury years back, to see if he would have a look at it. I went to see him and there wasn't really a conclusion: he just assumed that I might need a scan. Obviously for me at this point I had no club and was meant to be signing for Reading, so this was something I didn't have access to. He suggested that I needed to do Pilates which still now, to me, screams 'boring'. Still unaware of what the problem was, I was going on holiday with my family, and I decided to rest for a while to see if it helped the situation, which of course, it did. It started to feel much better after I had rested.

We came back from our holiday and soon after I was on my way to Reading with Dad to have my signing photos shot. I signed for Reading and was due to train the next day, still having visions of being able to come into a new environment and make an impression. I had my medical, which consisted of listing off all the injuries I've ever had. I always felt a bit embarrassed when it came to stuff like that. I always tried to laugh it off because the list, for my age, was a bit too long for my liking. Maybe people saw it as weak, I have no idea. I didn't really say much about my back though, as I clearly didn't think it was that bad and I also had no idea of what it could be. All I cared about was my new journey at my new club.

Training started and I managed to get myself through the first session; I don't remember having much pain at all, but in the gym session that followed, I do. As this progressed, I began to feel the pain in my back more every day. When I was running, jumping, landing, the pain was becoming more uncomfortable as it went on. I had been getting treatment on it so that I could try and get through training. To the physios, the symptoms I was describing sounded like a joint irritation, apparently. To me that didn't really mean anything though, as I was more worried about what people were going to think of me and how I was going to prove myself.

We were going to Holland for a pre-season tour and we were playing a friendly against Leicester the night before we travelled. The game was on a 3G pitch and we had just travelled up there on the bus. So, these are all reasons that may have contributed to why my back played up that day. During the warm-up I was in agony. We were then asked to do some work with higher speed and I physically could not break into a sprint because of the pain. I instantly pulled out, as to me something just didn't feel right. I could feel myself getting a bit worked up, as the last thing I wanted to do was pull out in the warm-up. I was then asked to do some band work to help activate my glutes to see if it made a difference. It did not. The staff let my manager know and she said she would only put me on if she desperately needed to. Inside I was hoping she didn't. I couldn't even sprint, it would have been a mockery.

We arrived in Holland and the problem persisted. I couldn't even do a warm-up without being in pain. This is when I really started to question what was going on. I would rest for a couple of days and then go back on the pitch and the back felt much better, but only for a short amount of time, then the pain would come back. It seemed to be a theme that was recurring; the more I rested, the better it felt. Still assuming it was a joint irritation, the physios carried on with this plan: treating it and resting it then getting me back on the pitch.

Not knowing what was wrong with my back meant I didn't hold back in my initiation at Reading. I always give my initiations 100 per cent. My song was Britney Spears' 'Toxic' and I really came with the moves. Twerking, sliding on the floor, I even sat on someone's lap. I was literally a few weeks in with this team, but I think a few of the girls got to know my personality for the first time that day. The Britney wig really came as a surprise for some. I still wanted to be myself and show that side of me even though deep down I was very stressed about the injury I could potentially have.

We had a friendly against Ajax on a boiling hot, beautiful day. We saw a couple of the men's team leaving the ground from their morning session, including Daley Blind.

During the warm-up I knew I wasn't right, but I kept telling myself it was alright, the physios were convinced it was fine for me to play on it and I wanted to believe it. I didn't want my mind to be focussed on the pain, I wanted to trust what they said. It was almost like telling yourself, 'stop being a pussy and push through it'.

I began to watch the game, visualising myself coming on and making a difference. I had the confidence that I could do bits in this team but the timing of this injury was poor. The level of coaching was high at Reading and the technical detail was crazy, I wasn't used to it. I came on for a few minutes, maybe ten or 15, I don't really remember, and I barely touched the ball. I tried to focus on appreciating being there, at the main Ajax training facilities. I did what I could, having barely been involved in training, and being in pain, but I just felt embarrassed deep down. It was too difficult to take on the technical and tactical detail while fighting the want/need to prove myself, while being in pain and in the unknown.

It was only when we arrived home from tour and started training again that I had to say something to the physios about my back, because to me it didn't feel like anything was getting better.

I honestly hated how it may have looked to people and I felt restricted, as the visions I had in my head about doing well just weren't happening. I couldn't play to any kind of potential. I started to feel like I was drifting further away from the team, and this is hard at any point for any person, but being a new signing and already being back in this position made it really hard to deal with. I'd come into a new environment, the manager had signed me because she saw something in me and I was unable to prove any of that because I had basically arrived at the club injured. It was even tougher because England's most capped player was in the team. She was a baller, someone I looked up to, alongside many other talents in that Reading team. I know she won't mind me saying, but Fara Williams always had something to say, the banter was always flying. I get it, of course I get it. But the thoughts in my head were flying too. I started to feel stuck again.

I genuinely felt like no one really believed what I was feeling. I knew the pain I was in and how uncomfortable it made me feel. Every shot I hit was like a sharp pin being pushed into that area. The banter from the players is always going around and most of the time I am involved with it, but the banter I was getting at this stage started to make me feel like even my team-mates didn't believe what I was feeling. This comes back to the thoughts I have and how I let them affect me. For me at the time it was just difficult, coming into a completely new environment with the injury history that I already had, to then be back in the same place with a different injury when I should have been thriving, learning, doing what I love.

Eventually it got to the point where I had to ask for a scan. I had to do something about what was going on. I didn't feel like it was getting better, I just had a gut feeling that there was something more going on in there. An MRI scan was arranged, and the results came soon after. The results were that I had a stress response on both sides of my lower back, L5 to be exact, but with the MRI not being able to show much else, a CT scan was arranged. By this point I felt like I had already started to accept what was going on. I was going to be out of football again and in this place that I know too well already.

It is so weird for me to say this but part of me hoped that the results came back showing something was wrong, because I thought no one believed me. How could the pain I was feeling come back as nothing? It was a very anxious period waiting for the results.

The results came back and revealed that I had a pars stress fracture in the left side of my back, L5. I answered the phone, listened to what the physio had to say, and it didn't really sink in until I came off the phone and told my parents the result. My dad seemed instantly affected by it. I had already missed pre-season with my new team, and now I was being told this. There was no start of the season for me. I was back in that place again. The frustration killed me.

How could I be back here again? Back on that lonely road to recovery. Why does this keep happening to me? All I want to do is play football. Any chance?

After the initial feeling of being absolutely gutted and feeling a bit sorry for myself, it didn't take me long to realise that this injury was different to the others in terms of the way I looked at it, the way I reacted to it. Yes, there were times when I was angry and frustrated but for the majority of the time I managed to stay positive and tried to put things into perspective. I know everyone has heard this saying, but I had to look at the bigger picture. When I had found out I was close to signing for Reading I couldn't believe it, I had felt very lucky to be there. Now, having signed a two-year deal, I knew that no matter how long it took to get it all right, I still had that second year. Another year, another chance to prove myself.

So, from then on it was all about that: every gym session, rehab session, whatever it was, it was to get closer to being in the right place to perform. I had to accept the time frame for which I was to be away from the pitch.

I started to learn a lot from that back injury: a huge part is learning to accept things as they are. The sooner I accepted what was going on, the easier it was for me to focus my attention on all the things I needed to do to get closer to getting back. Acceptance enables our mental state to contribute energy towards what we want to do or achieve, which means we will be more effective in doing so. Once we can see the positive that comes in the form of a negative, we are already winning in our minds. It is important to remember that staying in the right mindset is so key. It is important to recognise that timing is everything: some things take longer than expected, or don't go to plan, but trusting the process is vital, although it is easy to lose sight of that when your motivation and belief are constantly being tested.

But this injury was what made me realise I want to help people, whether it be the younger generation of female footballers, injured players or whoever else. During the writing of this book, I have learned so much about myself and so much about why I have experienced feeling the way I have, that I don't want to keep it quiet. I want to help people, by opening up in this book to the extent that I am, no matter how much it exposes me. We are human, we all experience terrible things in real life and terrible things in our heads. It is normal to have bad days, but I am writing this with the chance that someone may relate and be helped by me exposing parts of my journey.

Chapter Five

Facing a New Pressure

THROUGHOUT A football career or any career, we will all face different pressures or challenges. Up to this point in my career, around 2019, I had been dealing with the challenge of returning from injuries rather than the pressure of playing. These are different and I guess I found it hard to get my head around that.

I was in my early 20s and I was experiencing a completely different feeling/emotion to what I had had before in returning from an injury. I found myself fit and in full training with no restriction, which is something I hadn't been used to, especially with the level of the team I was playing with [Reading]. It was difficult to adjust my way of thinking. I was no longer worried about being injured and missing more football; I was now over-thinking my current situation which involved many different thoughts. I wanted to prove myself and I got frustrated because the problem with athletes, or even us as humans, is we are never content or happy with where we are: we naturally want to do better. I've found that for me it is almost an obsession. I am a perfectionist, so if things don't go right, I then put myself down, I think all sorts of things that eventually drag my performance down, and me as a person. Every thought leads down a different path and that tended to be something I would lose control of.

I went for a coffee with one of my team-mates just as we went into pre-season and I remember saying that I was just happy to be injury-free, and back out there on the pitch. I genuinely was just so excited, having worked so hard to get there. Looking back now, it was almost a bit naive of me because I wasn't really thinking about the competition I would face from other players, or what would happen when things didn't go right, the need to improve and get to the level I wanted to, or the level of the players around me. I wasn't thinking about what the manager might think of me, what my team-mates might think, but I should have been, because these are all reasons why we face a complete mental roller coaster almost every day as professional footballers.

There are a lot of demands we have to meet daily in this job and I found adjusting to that was tough, especially after having a long time out of the game. Like I mentioned, you have lost your sharpness physically, and need to get that back, but that's the part you can almost be okay with and accept. It's the mental side of things that begins to weigh you down. Being in that place and not knowing how to handle it or deal with it was quite stressful. You just must do the best you can to move forward and get on with it, while finding ways of helping with the lows, as we all know we can embrace the highs. It is important to deal with the lows, so that when they happen, we can carry on giving our best performances while experiencing them. Dwelling on things never helps anything. I tried not to show how I felt; there is that stigma in sport, especially football, that if you are struggling mentally then you are automatically seen as weak. You are afraid the manager won't trust you or play you if you admit it.

In March 2019 I saw a story in the news about a young footballer, Joel Darlington, who had taken his own life after suffering from persistent injury problems which had halted his progress within the game. He was 20.

The majority of footballers start playing when they are a kid. It's just a fun game that we fall in love with. As we get older it is no longer 'just' football: it is now a business, with money involved, pressure involved, image, media, stats … It changes the way we look at ourselves, think of ourselves and in a lot of cases this is a negative change.

No one can have known exactly what was going through Joel's head throughout his struggle, but he was suffering with injuries which could have been the beginning of it for him. Do we as footballers get so caught up in this career that we forget there is more to us than football? We sacrifice so much of our lives for it, but actually, we have so much more depth than just being a football player. Do young players who are trying to build a football career lose sight of this?

We will all face different pressures or challenges during our careers and in 2019 I was having to deal with the challenges of playing regularly, injury-free and at a high level, for the first time. This was a different pressure to before: incomparable in fact.

As a professional player, your career is essentially in someone else's hands when it comes to contracts, game time, days off, loading etc. There is plenty that is out of our control and that is an unsettling feeling for some people a lot of the time, especially when things aren't going the way we want or 'need' them to be going. This isn't unique to football: it is the same in many careers. It is down to the individual to try their best to adjust to the environment around them and to do what the manager and coaches want. I became too invested in worrying about what they wanted from me, how they wanted me to play, specific movements and passes. I felt I lost myself a little bit as a player, which leads to a lack of confidence. As soon as I felt like I wasn't being the best I could be, I would allow it to drag me down. I would over-think, obsess, and dwell. This all led to an unhealthy mind and I found it quite hard to bounce back from that. Of course, we also have things happening in our lives outside of football, like relationships, that contribute to this kind of feeling. It can all come to a head, and it is not an easy place to come out of.

In January 2020, Reading had an FA Cup fourth-round game at London City Lionesses who played in the league below us, and I was in the starting 11. I was excited to start the game, but something just didn't really feel right. I know how it feels to be excited to play and this feeling just wasn't the same. Something was off. I didn't feel right in my head and it was after this game that it all started to become very apparent to me that your mindset is probably the biggest and most important part of your game.

In the weeks before the game I had been struggling with my anxiety, due to relationship reasons, and this wasn't something I could just turn on and off at the time, so going into the game itself my head hadn't been in the right place for a while. My feelings were almost at an 'I give up' stage and it really showed during the game.

For me, even though I knew I wasn't in a great place in my head, I still put myself under the pressure of wanting to prove myself and perform, execute the game plan, do everything we practised in the week leading up to the game. It was a fixture that I was expected to do well in, as it was against opposition from the league below, a game I was probably expected to score in. But where did those expectations come from? The coaches, or me? This is something worth thinking about.

The game started and it was going fine. The thing is when you play in a team, you get voices coming from everywhere: from the bench, the management area and of course your own. During the game I could feel myself

My brain (mind)

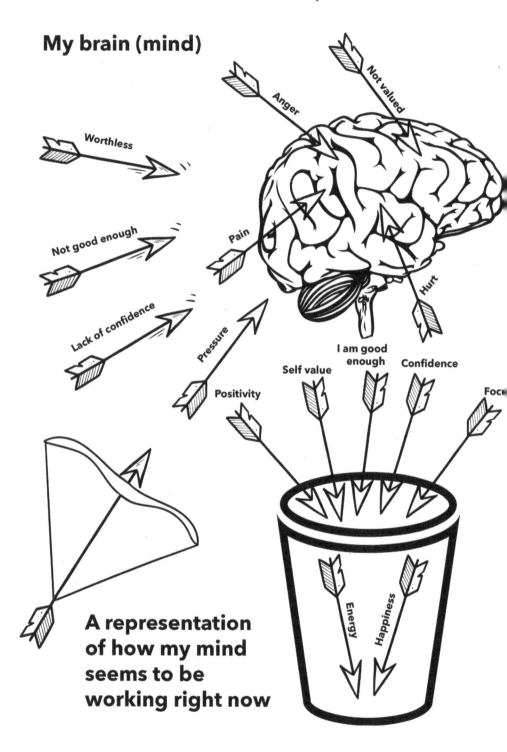

A representation of how my mind seems to be working right now

falling to pieces mentally. I got 'the breathing thing' which hadn't happened to me for a long time and that in itself was enough to send my head crazy; it shocked my system. The anxiety while playing is horrible and I then lost control of my thoughts. Everything that entered my head was negative. I could feel myself deteriorating, mentally, on the pitch and again, it showed. What is in your head always feels worse to you than how someone would view it looking in, but all I can say is that on that day I didn't play like myself at all. I don't know who was on that pitch to be honest.

I saw my parents in the crowd and I nearly burst into tears wondering what they thought of this shit show. But I kept pulling myself through. The whistle blew and we had won the game with ease, but it just felt horrible. I was trying to hold every emotion that I was feeling inside, and when the team talk finished, I went straight over to my parents and broke down in their arms crying. There were players, fans and staff that could all see it, but in that moment I didn't care. I didn't want to feel like that. Why did I feel like that? I hated myself for feeling that way. I was embarrassed.

That same day it came out that Kobe Bryant had been killed in a helicopter accident, and it instantly put things into perspective for me. When you find yourself in a hole that you don't feel like you can come out of, it is sometimes hard to see perspective and it often comes unexpectedly. Should we look to put things into perspective when we feel down?

Kobe was not only a worldwide star because of being an idolised basketball player, he was also very well known for the positivity that he spread with the things he said and did. I don't know that much about him to be honest, but a video I watched after finding out the news of his death really opened my eyes.

If you want to watch the video, search 'Kobe Bryant, the Mindset of a Winner' on YouTube.

Some of the important messages that Kobe put across in this video are:

'The greatest fear we have is ourselves'.

'I'm not afraid to fail.'

'Be still and understand that things come and go, emotions come and go – the important thing is to accept them all, to embrace them all and then you can choose to do with them what you want versus being controlled by emotion.'

'Be able to look at it for what it is, which is really your imagination running its course.'

It seems simple doesn't it, to tell yourself to put things into perspective, but it isn't always as easy as it sounds. In a moment when everything feels like it is crashing down, how do you just switch on that mindset, how do you look at the bigger picture in those moments that seem the hardest? The reality of the situation now is that I had a bad game against London City Lionesses. So what? Everyone has a bad game.

Chapter Six

OCD

YOU HAVE probably heard someone say they have OCD at some point in your life; it is quite commonly said, in my experience anyway. I do believe that most people have some sort of OCD (obsessive-compulsive disorder) trait, or hints of it during anxious times in their lives. But I guess it isn't OCD until it genuinely affects your life and the way you live it.

I suffer from OCD. I was diagnosed with it at the age of 14, I think. It is an anxiety disorder in which people have unwanted and repeated thoughts, feelings, images, and sensations (obsessions) and engage in behaviours or mental acts in response to them. Often the person carries out the behaviours to reduce the impact or get rid of the thought. It's hard to try and get to the bottom of why a disorder like this can come about for someone. It could be down to your genes: I recently found out that my grandma (we called her 'grandma poorly legs') was believed to have suffered with OCD.

The first memory I have of my OCD was when I was in year five at school. I was going to go on a school trip and be away for a few nights. I can remember feeling the urge to make sure my bedroom was spotless, everything put in place, everything tidy and in order. If it felt like something was out of place, I would rearrange it until it felt better. I'm pretty sure I even hoovered my mattress.

Imagine having a voice in your head that is constantly telling you what to do and dictating how you are going to feel if you do not listen to it.

OCD can start when someone is anxious about something, which leads them to behave the way they do. In most cases of OCD, the individual will get anxious about something and then feel the urge to perform a ritual; they may also get thoughts that if they don't perform the ritual then something bad could happen. (For example, a family member could get hurt if they weren't to perform the ritual in mind.)

For me, it was the opposite. I knew that if I didn't do what it wanted me to do that nothing bad was going to happen. After suffering for a long while, I knew that my thoughts were irrational and ridiculous, but the voice/urge was too strong for me not to listen to it, which is why it ended up getting bad. If I was to list some of the things that would go through my mind and some of the things I had to do to make the uncomfortable feeling go away, you wouldn't believe.

Adults with OCD spend a lot of time and effort trying to avoid things which trigger their symptoms. You might avoid shaking hands with people or, if you are afraid of harming people, you might avoid using scissors or knives. People with OCD use distraction to shift attention away from their obsessions by thinking about or doing something else. They also get family and friends involved by making them live by certain 'rules', for example asking them to change out of their 'dirty' clothes as soon as they get home.

So, having OCD doesn't only make it hard for the person who has it, it also makes things very hard for the people close to that individual. Some of the rituals/actions that I used to perform would also be forced upon my partner or family members. I found that hard to deal with and found myself apologising a lot and getting extremely embarrassed, because I knew the thoughts I was having were irrational – but that didn't stop the fact that I had to do what the OCD was telling me to do.

'Rule your mind, or it will rule you' – Horace.

As you can imagine my OCD really affected me in everyday life: school, playing football, work, going out with friends. It was just everywhere I went, and I couldn't seem to go anywhere without the stress of my OCD. I saw three different counsellors to try and help with it. It used to get to a point where I felt I could control it and keep on top of it, but then it would always spiral out of control again. I ended up adjusting my life because of my OCD. Thinking back now,

I may have stopped the counselling because it was getting close to the point where I had to face it and try and fight it and I just couldn't do it. So, I would convince myself that I had it all under control.

I used to avoid things that would trigger it or certain people who would set it off because I couldn't stand the hassle of listening to my thoughts. I would anticipate what my OCD would tell me to do, so to prevent it, I would just avoid a lot of situations that would trigger my OCD. Even the thought of being in those uncomfortable situations would upset me.

OCD quickly became a massive part of my life as I started to get older. From being an anxious child during football matches getting 'the breathing thing', I was showing other signs of anxiety such as in primary school when I used to go on sleepovers at friends' houses. It would get to a point in the evening, and I would just want to go home because I felt so anxious. There were times when I made myself sick so they would call my parents to come and pick me up. That was usually my excuse, that I wasn't feeling very well. I don't remember why I used to feel that way, but I just did.

When my OCD started to get severely worse, I was in secondary school. I remember doing silly little things, like if I crossed a word out then it had to be crossed out five times or scribbled out one, two, three, four, five times. Or sometimes if I made just one mistake in my book, I would have to rip the whole page out and start again. This was obviously that perfectionist trait and as you can imagine when you're trying to learn and take everything in, this was a very frustrating thing to deal with. I found myself not listening in class because I was too focussed on what was going on in my head or feeling like I needed to get up and wash my hands because I had touched something I felt was dirty. I always ended up watching people do things that would trigger me, and I used to get so angry about it: why did I have to see that and now I have to go and fucking sort myself out, wash my hands or stay away from them. A list would start to be created in my head, for example things I had to wash when I got home – items of clothing or myself. If something was missed off the list then I would most likely have to do it all again.

As time has gone by, the experiences I've had with OCD have been different, the rituals have changed a lot and the intrusive thoughts have changed. Most of the time it was linked to cleanliness but I also experienced other things for shorter amounts of time, like if my left elbow banged on something then I had to do the same on the other side to even it out or I wouldn't feel right. This applied to all body parts.

During school the worst one for me was a problem I used to have with one of my classmates. For some reason in my mind (it could have been something that I heard about her that I then believed) I had convinced myself that she was dirty – she wasn't clean and if I touched her or touched something/someone she may have touched then I would also be dirty, or 'contaminated' is the word I used when I spoke about it with my counsellor at the time. Because of what was in my head, it made my world at school extremely stressful and sometimes unbearable.

This was when my obsession with hand sanitiser and cleanliness started. In case this girl had touched any handles in the school, (it could have been anything that was a shared surface) I would use my sleeve to open any doors or kick open doors or even wait for others to go through a door, so I didn't need to touch the handle. To help with this I started to carry around hand sanitiser with me everywhere I went and would also wash my hands a lot more than the average person to try and make myself feel better about it. It was so extreme that sometimes I had to put the hand sanitiser on my face, on my skin and in my hair as the contamination may have been there. I would get through packets of anti-bac wipes. These were the levels I would go to, to try and get rid of the intrusive thoughts. It was so extreme that even the thought of being 'contaminated' would get to me so much I would become quite emotional and overwhelmed. I let this get so out of control that I noticed myself focussing on the things that should not have mattered – things like being aware of what she was touching to make sure I didn't touch it or even who she may have made contact with, so I knew to avoid them. The number of times I would come home from school and put my blazer through the wash to basically clear my conscience was ridiculous and it definitely sent my mum up the wall. I still to this day don't really know what it was about this girl that set my OCD off so much, but since then I have come across a few people that have affected it in the same way.

Another massive part of what triggered my OCD is really embarrassing for me to admit for some reason. But I used to have a serious problem with periods. Periods were my worst nightmare at one stage, I couldn't hack anybody talking about them because of the thoughts it started in my head. For me, if someone told me they were on their period, my world would instantly come crashing down. It would start a maze of intrusive thoughts that would include: have they washed their hands properly? What if they didn't wash their hands after they went to the toilet? The washing hands one was massive for me because I have witnessed so many people use the bathroom and not wash their hands afterwards. Even if I didn't have OCD, I would still think that was wrong, though.

There are two examples I can think back to that I can vividly remember. As football started to get more serious, I began to get called up to England camps. For me this was a very anxious experience in itself, because I wanted to do well. I wanted to prove myself and show everyone the reason why I was called up. I wanted it to be the perfect experience. This was made way more difficult while my OCD was bad. OCD gets worse depending on how you feel, so the fact that I was nervous and anxious about the camp only made matters worse. Anyway, I started to feel the same way about one of the girls at camp as I had about the girl from school. I would go away with England, which should be a very proud and exciting moment as a young footballer aspiring to be a professional, but instead for me it was a mental battle. I would turn up to camp praying that I wouldn't be roomed with this individual because I wouldn't have been able to handle the way it made me feel. So instead of trying to be calm and relaxed and focussing on the training sessions and actually being on an England camp, my mind would be completely elsewhere, focussing on all the wrong things.

I can remember we got a coach to training and I would be looking around to see where she was so I didn't put my things near hers. I actually think she may have asked me to put her GPS unit into the back of her shirt once, but I made an excuse and said I needed to tie my shoelaces or something. Thinking back to this it actually makes me feel so silly to think that I was acting this way but in that moment that's what was real for me.

I can also remember that she was on her period and she, like a lot of girls probably do, was paranoid that she had 'leaked'. So, she asked a few of us who were behind her 'have I leaked?' For most girls, this was a simple question which they would have answered and got on with their day, but for me this meant that another wave of anxiety had come through me, and I had to try and act like it hadn't because we had training and I needed to focus on doing well. Then the obsessive thoughts would happen; for the remainder of the camp I would be even more switched on but for the wrong reasons. I would try and avoid touching anything she may have touched; this was made difficult as we obviously had meal times together and it was a buffet-style dinner, meaning everybody touches the serving spoons etc. Luckily for me, there was always hand sanitiser out at mealtimes which practically saved my head in this situation. Of course, I had a back-up in my pocket anyway as I needed to be prepared. The thing is, anybody on camp could have been on their period but if I didn't know about it then it didn't matter as much.

Being called up to a camp is initially a very happy and proud moment, but that feeling never lasted for long because it was soon overtaken by anxiety. One of the worst times I can remember was when I was so anxious about being roomed with the girl who I saw as being 'dirty' that I would cry about it. The car journey on the way to a camp was the worst; I always wished that it would never end because the longer I was in the car, the less time I would have to be at camp with my OCD all over the place. When you arrive at camp, the first thing that happens is you fill out a couple of forms and then find out your room-mate. Sometimes room-mates stayed the same but they also changed a lot. It was the moment I was dreading, I tried to reassure myself the whole time leading up to it: well, there's 20-odd girls on this camp, what are the chances I'll room with her? Anyway, the worst possible thing for me happened that day. I was assigned to room with her. As soon as I found out I was really uncomfortable and overwhelmed. I couldn't do it; there is no way I could room with this girl. I had to tell someone. So, I pulled the strength and conditioning coach to one side and I nearly had a breakdown to him, (I think he could tell that I was quite distressed) saying that they had to change my room-mate. I could see he didn't really know how to react as I was clearly in a bit of a state about it. Anyway, he asked me who I would like to room with and I said a girl who I had roomed with a few times before, so thankfully he made that happen for me and they acted like they made a mistake with the rooms and changed a couple of them around. So, the camp didn't start off great for me personally and I was pretty anxious throughout.

I tried my very best to get on with everything and do what was expected of me in terms of the training and everything else that happens on camp, but I could never switch off. I could never relax from my thoughts. It was constant. During a training session I could feel myself struggling more and more in my head, pushing myself down further and further. I eventually pulled myself out of a session and used a recent hip problem as an excuse. Later that day I was in my room with my room-mate and she told me that her period had started and it was really heavy. I could feel my mind filling up and my emotions going out of control and I couldn't handle it anymore in that moment. I took myself out the room straight

About ten years old with my team Portsmouth Ladies

FA Youth Cup Final after getting substituted off injured. Age 15

School photo

Cosham Blues celebrating a goal

Playing for my first ever team, Cosham Blues

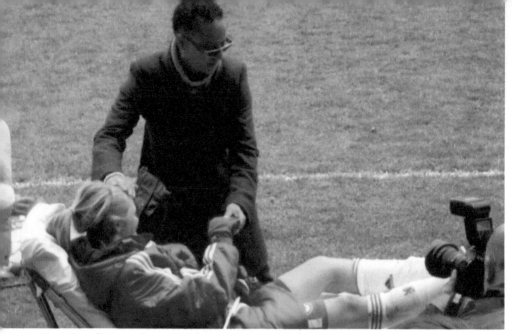

Hope Powell presenting me with my winners' medal

Lifting the FA Youth Cup before being taken to hospital

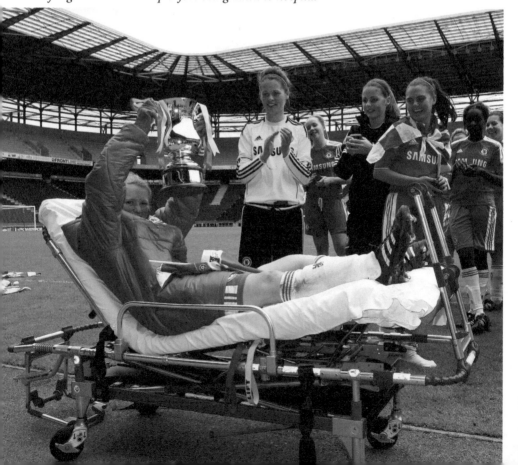

Team photo from the FA Youth Cup Final after beating Arsenal

Age 16. Post-surgery in hospital

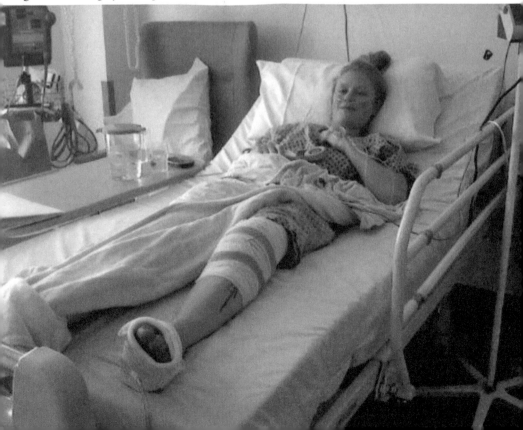

Celebrating my first goal for Chelsea's first team before going pro

Bristol City in 2016, the first shoulder dislocation

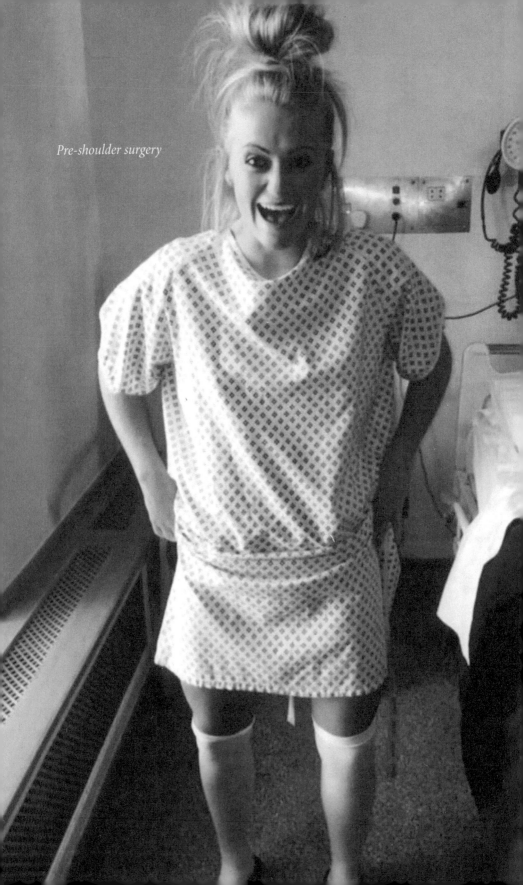

Pre-shoulder surgery

away to see the doctor who was on camp and I cried my eyes out to him about my OCD. I'm not going to lie, to this day I don't believe that he understood, but how could he? I didn't even understand and I was the one experiencing it.

I decided to speak to the head coach on the camp, Mo Marley, and I tried to explain to her what was going on. I also told her that I was going to sort it out. I was sat there with someone who is there to judge me on my footballing ability and there was me struggling with my own mental issues. I hated it. I hated how it made me feel, I hated how it affected my football and most of all I hated how I felt it affected the people around me. I later got sent home from the camp as I couldn't deal with being there anymore. I think I used the hip problem as part of the reason so it didn't look as bad, as people got sent home from camps all the time with physical injuries, but when it comes to something mental, to me it could have seemed to come across as 'weak', which of course it is not, but people that don't understand this kind of thing automatically think that's the case.

The fact that the way my OCD made me feel could lead to such dramatic outcomes really got to me. The level of embarrassment and disappointment in myself was tough. It was also terrible how it affected the people around me. I almost became some sort of 'police' at home, to the point of making certain family members wash their hands if we had been out somewhere and I had seen one of them touch something that may have triggered it off. We could be out somewhere and my mood could completely change because someone had done something that set thoughts off, something I thought they could have avoided. It was utterly irrational but real life for me. In my eyes the sooner something was washed, the better, because that meant it couldn't be spread as far.

I went to a friend's house party. We were in my friend's room and I was sat in her bed. When I moved, I noticed a stain that had probably been there for a while. This instantly took me over and all I had rushing through my head was 'it must be period blood' and so on and so on. I stayed the night and slept in a different bed but could not stop thinking about it; it had taken over my mind. I was the first one awake in the morning and it was early, maybe like 6am. I decided to sneak out of the house alone, and walk all the way home in my pyjamas. It was just over a four-mile walk so it took me about an hour and a half. When I got home, I think my family were still sleeping because I had left my friend's house that early. I found the spare key and let myself in the back door, remembering everything I had touched so I could go back and clean it until I was satisfied. I felt so disgusting that everything I had worn had to go in the wash, I had to shower thoroughly and clean every item I had with me at the party. But it didn't stop there. Of course, I had to anti-bac every door handle I touched when coming back into my house, including the key I used to get back in. It was like I was some sort of criminal trying to hide my tracks and not leave any kind of evidence.

The lengths I would go to, to make the thoughts go away, were ridiculous. It actually makes me feel so ashamed and embarrassed to write about it now. I had so little control over it, that I was willing to do anything to feel better about it. There were even times that I was convinced the washing machine was dirty so I would put a wash on to clean it before it cleaned my clothes. Makes sense, no?

Obviously, what I'm telling you now is just a glimpse of what I went through. So, as you can probably picture, as my life went on and I got a bit older, this obsessive-compulsive disorder made everything I did a million times harder. You might think it sounds very intense and even me reading this back puts me in disbelief that it was at this level. The thing is, I could go through every ritual that my OCD told me to do, and it still wouldn't be good enough, it wouldn't be clean enough. Sometimes I just had to keep cleaning until I felt better.

The way it used to make me react made me so ashamed of myself, I would get to a point where it built up so much that I just broke down. The anger and aggression that it used to cause was horrible. The anger would be aimed at an individual if something they did could have triggered it all off in my head. I hated myself for this. I saw myself as weak because I could not stop it from controlling me.

The outbursts could lead to punching walls, crying my eyes out hysterically, shouting 'fuck off' to my OCD at the top of my voice, because I couldn't handle it. I couldn't handle how it made me feel. I just wanted it to go away.

It often made me feel like a controlling weirdo, when I would tell a family member to wash their hands or whatever it may have been. There were extremes, when I would see them touch something when we were out and then, after they had driven home, I would be straight back out to the car with the anti-bac wipes to clean everything that may have been touched. Even in front of my family I was so embarrassed that a lot of the time I would try and hide the fact that I had gone to clean something. Sometimes I would sneak out to do it while they were watching TV so they wouldn't ask me questions about it.

I always found myself saying sorry because I knew it was ridiculous and it wasn't normal, but I just couldn't help it.

I couldn't even do something normal like bowling without there being a problem. I was with my sister and her boyfriend and my girlfriend at the time. Thinking about it now, a bowling alley is not the most hygienic place to be, when all sorts of people's fingers have been in every single hole of every single ball. One time, there were two people bowling next to us and when the balls were returned to us by the machine, you could end up with any ball on your side of it. The entire time I couldn't switch off because I saw them as dirty and I had all sorts of scenarios going through my mind. By the end of the game, I had to make everyone go and wash their hands, otherwise I would make a note in my head of everything they had touched (handles or whatever) and I would have to clean all of that as well.

So, by making them wash their hands, I saved myself a lot of energy and stress.

When I moved to Bristol on loan in 2016, I knew my situation regarding my head. I was going to be living in a club house, with other players, and I had a conversation with the manager Willie Kirk before I moved as I was so anxious about my OCD kicking off and me ending up embarrassing myself. I explained that I had OCD and asked whether it would be okay for me to have the room with the en suite. If he was unaware of what OCD was, he probably thought I was being a princess wanting the room with the bathroom. I didn't even want to know what the girls might have thought – some girl coming in on loan from Chelsea demanding the best room in the house?! Ha ha.

When I think about the way I used to be when my OCD was at its worst, it makes me sad and angry, that I let a little voice in my head tell me what to do. I am so furious that I wasn't in control of my mind. I couldn't do what I wanted to do or act like a 'normal' person sometimes. It took over my life.

Of course, it wasn't like that all the time. There were times where I felt like I could keep it under control but there were also times when I couldn't. I would want or need to focus on something else that was important so I would just listen to what it was telling me to do so I could get on with my life without having these impeding thoughts constantly in my head.

As an athlete naturally we put ourselves under pressure and I feel that this had a large effect on the severity of my OCD. That is why I was so bad on England camps. I used to get so worked up beforehand, my OCD would go through the roof leading up to it and during it. When I got home, I used to be so mentally drained. My mind would never rest, it was 24/7 constant stress and worry. This is no way to live.

This takes me back to the importance of recognising struggle and being able to deal with it. When I was going through my second ACL recovery, my OCD was pretty bad because I was already going through the mental/physical battle of returning from this injury. Because I wanted to focus on my return to play and recovery from the injury, I just let my OCD get out of control again because facing it was too hard. But what we all know is that if we don't face our fears then we will never overcome them or be stronger than them.

Many of us footballers like to feel that football is everything. It's not, and it is important for us to realise this. There is more to life than football. It's about ultimately being happy and if we are, we can accomplish anything. Happiness is the ultimate power and key to living our best life. When life is good and injury-free and when we are performing, we don't tend to think about things like this, but during the long period of time I have spent away from the pitch already in my short career, I have learned to appreciate many things. Even when I'm not playing football – when I'm in what we would call boring rehab – I appreciate the position I'm in. I appreciate my family and friends and I feel happy. I feel happy because I have the ability to look at things in a different light, in a way that means I can still take positives from the negative of not playing. I still believe in my ability – being injured just means we can work on many other things that we weren't good at before, get stronger (mentally and physically).

If I am happy, I can perform better; if I am relaxed, then I will perform better.

During my long periods of being injured, I have felt very pointless and this is partly why I've chosen to write this book. I want to share my experiences, thoughts, and story with others who may be going through similar things.

I've always been able to cover up how much my OCD would affect me. There were a few times in my shared house that they would see how much it affected me but when I left the house and went to football I would always be able to hide it. I would say I'm quite a loud and bubbly person so if I showed how it was making me feel, then it would be easy to notice. I hid it well and only the closest people to me and my family would know how much I used to struggle.

In 2018 I took a turn for the better mentally. I had just come back from a very challenging injury and when I signed for my new club (a permanent contract at Bristol) me and my partner at the time split up. This was yet another thing I had to deal with on top of what I had just been through;

it just felt like one thing after another. Now, I am mentally stronger than I have ever been, but that is because of what I have been through on my journey of life until this point. It has taught me so much about myself and about how to deal with and react to things.

The lows I experienced while having OCD mean it is something I would never wish upon anybody, but my experience of OCD has actually taught me so much and has helped me realise so much. We are a product of our own thoughts. How many thoughts go through our heads every day? Hundreds and thousands. It is down to us which ones we listen to and which ones we don't but it is how they affect us that matters. How we let them get to us and how we deal with them. Imagine every thought we get is a cloud passing by in the sky on a sunny/cloudy day. The world doesn't stop turning, the clouds pass by and pass by.

If only it was that simple for us, as OCD sufferers, but it is not. Each cloud of thought that may pass through our head could be full of intrusive, negative, unhealthy thoughts which can spiral out of control for many of us. This can lead to suffering from anxiety and even depression.

My point is that thoughts aren't real. They can come from a very deep place and they are enforced by our ego. This is something I have learned recently. Our ego is what needs and wants. When I injured my knee, I was able to go for a scan which could tell me the facts, it could tell me exactly what was going on inside my knee, exactly what damage had been done, because it is something we can physically see. However, if I were to go for a scan on my head, would the results come back showing me that my thoughts were real or that I was suffering with OCD, or anxiety? Absolutely not, because the thoughts are not real. The place that they have come from could be based on true events but the actual thoughts themselves are not real – yet they have the ability to make us feel the way that they do, whether it's positive or negative.

We have the ability to believe anything. Many of us grew up believing that a man with a long white beard, dressed in a red and white outfit who is slightly overweight, manages to fit down a chimney along with a big brown sack every year to deliver presents to children all over the world in just one night. I believed this and for many years it brought me and my brother and sister so much joy. We believed so deeply that we were convinced we could hear him that night while he snuck in to give us what we had hoped for at Christmas. We lost sleep over the excitement and couldn't believe our eyes when half a carrot and crumbs of a mince pie remained from what we had left out for him. I actually remember my sister waking up to my mum filling her stocking but my mum managed to save herself by saying she was seeing what Santa had brought her this year. Of course, my sister believed her and went back to sleep. All of that to then find out eventually that he doesn't actually exist. The same goes for the tooth fairy and the Easter bunny. It is mad to think that we were okay with the thought of all these strange but interesting characters just entering our houses while we were sleeping, to do their job. It is a belief system. When we believe something, it becomes real and we attach emotions and feelings to it. The reality is that we are responsible for our emotions and other people/things don't make us feel anything. They are just circumstances we have thoughts about and end up believing and that then leads to emotions and if this is out of control or not managed properly it is a very difficult place to be.

I have experienced very negative and very intrusive thoughts and they have affected me deeply because of the emotions that are attached to them. It is only since I started to realise that they are not real that I have been able to be more at peace with myself.

The more we believe in something, the more real it will seem to us. It is crazy how powerful the brain is, but a lot of the time it is powerful for the wrong reasons. We are not our thoughts. My OCD had the capability to lead me to believe what I was thinking and feeling was real when it wasn't. It was made up in my head and was irrational. But because I was unable to control or understand or deal with the thoughts, I let them take over. What I am talking about doesn't only come in the form of OCD. Every day we all have thoughts that we hold on to but this goes back to what I have learned about ego and belief systems.

I still have OCD and I will always have it but it is nowhere near as bad as it used to be. I have got to a point where I understand it and I am able to deal with it and control it so much better, which means life in general is made easier. Instead of going into my thoughts, I try to observe them for what they are: only thoughts.

As my life with OCD has gone on, I have obviously gone through stages of being able to cope with it and not being able to cope with it very well. This is massively influenced by how I feel at the time, so for example if my emotions are running high then my OCD is most likely to be quite bad. The longer you have it, I guess the more you learn about it. So, for me I have ways of coping with it, which actually means the effort I used to have to go through in terms of rituals, is no longer as much effort for me because I'm used to it. I am used to the way it is for me, so I find myself doing things to avoid the feeling. I have my own way of coping. This is by no means normal. If I were to write down all of the things I have to do or things I avoid and told a 'normal' person they had to live by these rules for one day, I'm sure it would exhaust them and they would find it extremely strange, but to me it isn't an effort anymore because I am so used to what I need to do and the way things need to be for me to be a bit more chilled out.

It might feel like time helps us heal from things but all it really does is teach us to live with the issue. When you do something or behave a certain way for so long this becomes normal for you and becomes less draining. This does not mean the issue has gone away, you have just adjusted to it and ingrained it into your life. If you do not address the problem, then it will simply remain there. It will continue to repeat itself.

My dad Keith has some thoughts to share on what it has been like dealing with my OCD:

'While they were hard to accept, the physical injuries Millie had were easy to understand,' he says. 'Something was broken that needed fixing, rehab started and the journey began towards fitness and the resumption of Millie's playing career.

'Millie's OCD and anxiety has, in some respects, been more difficult to accept, and of course the treatment and recovery journey cannot be as easily defined.

'Most people have some awareness of OCD, although it is often restricted to the general association with the need for constant hand-cleaning etc. I was probably of that mindset before Millie's diagnosis, although I have since learned more about the hugely negative impact it can have on many aspects of someone's life.

'The term has also crept into everyday language; we have all overheard conversations where people describe themselves as "so OCD" when talking about relative normalities in life. In fairness it is probably only when someone close to you suffers from OCD that you start to pay attention and understand the detail and effects.

'I am by no means an expert in the subject, but it strikes me that someone suffering from OCD effectively has two brains. Obviously, they only have one, but the illness changes the decisions of the sufferer and the outcomes as follows:

1. Logical brain – The one that makes rational decisions.
2. OCD brain – The one that takes over the logical brain and insists that the sufferer follow its path or there will be dire consequences.

'Millie has described OCD as a voice in her head that constantly bangs on, insistently telling her to react in a certain way. Initially it is very hard to relate to this concept as a non-sufferer: I can remember telling her to ignore the symptoms as they were clearly not reality. With hindsight this was futile and stemmed from my lack of understanding and experience.

'There have been many occasions where OCD has taken over Millie's life. It is not for me to describe the effect that they have had on Millie; all I can say is that it's never positive and always damaging. OCD seems to block out any positive experience of a situation and replaces it with negativity and fear.

'Undoubtedly OCD and anxiety has had a negative effect on Millie's football career, and when heaped on top of the physical injuries she has suffered, it is amazing that she has achieved the levels she has and hopefully will do in the future. She has the tools and experience to overcome or at least manage the situation in the future, both in her sporting career and beyond.

'Mental illness is indeed an illness! It is just very difficult to understand and relate to it, particularly when someone close to you is the sufferer. I come from a generation where the subject was not a reality for many and was brushed under the carpet. As a nation we are still well behind the curve in understanding and dealing with the whole subject of mental health. I still have conversations with friends where they effectively deny that it exists, and say that "people should pull themselves together like they did in our day", or they should exercise "mental strength" to overcome it.'

And this is from my mum, Nikki:

'The earliest signs of Millie's anxiety were probably when she was around the age of eight or nine; she would go to a friend's house for a sleepover and we would be called to come and collect her as she had been sick. At first you don't really think too much of it, as some children just struggle with being away from home, but this became a real issue later on for Millie when she was selected for England camps. Although she was very excited to be selected, her anxiety would hinder her whole experience, which was very sad to witness as a parent; something which is supposed to be a positive experience turns into a traumatic one.

'As Millie started getting older, she started showing signs of OCD by continually asking me a question and then I would have to keep repeating the answer to her, which was quite frustrating, as I thought she was just trying to wind me up. However, now I understand this was Millie needing reassurance because she was feeling stressed about something. Following on from that came the continuous hand-washing and making everything just so in her bedroom before she had a football match.

'Things got progressively worse with having to sanitise the bottom of shoes, or bags, or anything that may have been in contact with anyone Millie deemed unclean. We tried to reason and rationalise these actions with Millie but it was like banging your head against a brick wall: none of it made sense in her mind; she had to carry out these rituals to make her feel better.

'Finally, at the age of about 14 when I could see how distressed she had become and how it was affecting her life, we contacted the doctor. After a consultation she was put in touch with a therapist who started to help her make sense of things.

'It's very heartbreaking to see your child go through such mental distress and not being able to stop it and make it better, as you know it's all in her mind and not something physical you can see.

'Also, I think as parents you can blame yourself for why your child has a mental health issue, going back in the past trying to work out how it could have manifested. You can ask yourself many questions: was it something we said to her as a child that caused it, was it because she had a grandmother who suffered from severe mental health issues or was it my own issues with anxiety that rubbed off on her? I have come to the conclusion that you can't try and put a finger on it or blame anyone for it. Everyone has their issues to deal with and not everyone's brains are wired the same way. All we can do is be understanding and supportive and not try to cover things up. It's not something to be ashamed or embarrassed about with family and friends; we should make people aware so they talk about it the same as you would a broken arm or leg.'

Chapter Seven

Anxiety and Relationships

I'VE FOUND that the stresses of football have also affected my relationships with people outside of football. It is so hard to be a full-time footballer with OCD and the added pressure I put on myself in the challenges I face daily, while also having a relationship outside of that. I know that I have taken out the emotions and feelings that I felt while injured on the closest person to me.

Even when I was finally fit and playing injury-free, I still found it difficult as I would put tremendous amounts of pressure on myself to perform or I would make comparisons to players I was competing with in my position and also over-think how I played or performed way too much. This starts off a pattern of negative thinking that continuously goes round in circles.

We are all experiencing things every day but sometimes it is too easy for me to let my moods and my actions be dictated by my past experiences or fears. Naturally, if we have been hurt in the past or injured, for example, our brain associates things that happen with feelings, which I feel can lead us to behave in a certain way and can also make us feel unpleasant emotions and thoughts.

I have actually found that the mentality I have had in the past, towards football or anything to do with football, has led me to be taken over by it.

When I have been injured, I know I have had to tick certain boxes to reach the next stage of my rehab or reach certain targets before I can progress. There is a guided plan of action which you must follow in order to reach the next stage, so to a certain extent it is controlled. The outcome is out of your control but there is a plan to follow. When I am fit and playing, I feel everything is more out of my control. What happens to you lies completely in the hands of the manager and coaching staff; all you can do is try your hardest to impress, work hard, do well in training. That is why it is so easy for me to put that pressure on myself, constantly wondering what they are thinking about me and my performances.

Anxiety – that horrible tight feeling in your chest, the deep, dark thoughts that make you feel like you're almost out of breath. The thoughts drag you down so low that you feel drained. You feel unhappy.

These thoughts are by no means necessarily true but when I believe them, it's a dark place to be. At times I believe the constant noise that has filled my head. I believe the thoughts so much that it creates pain and unhappiness inside me which lead to emotions that might result in an outburst or an unpleasant reaction towards others.

The thing is with my anxiety, I know the thoughts that I'm getting are not true, they are irrational, but yet I still listen to them, I still let them control my feelings. Because the truth is, I don't know how to deal with it, I don't know how to stop it from making me feel worthless or unhappy when I get terrible thoughts.

I have plenty of things to be happy about but a recent realisation that I have had has opened my eyes and made me understand that the anxiety has been a huge problem of mine for a long time. Yes, I've had counselling for my OCD, which of course is very much linked to anxiety, but this feels different. What I'm feeling is the same feeling I would get when certain things would happen in my relationship for example, where thoughts would come into my head about not being good enough, trust issues, insecurity issues. Basically, every situation that was out of my control would set me and my thoughts off on what I would call a mental roller coaster.

Of course, these thoughts can be triggered by something but it's what it can lead to which needs to be stopped. But it helps to try and figure out where this may be coming from. My guess is when I am in a relationship and feeling that way, my brain has probably linked what is happening to something from the past that led me to feel a certain way, and it becomes very overwhelming. The result is unhappiness towards myself, not forever but for a period of time. It is like finding comfort in insecurity and that's not healthy.

I find it hard to make those thoughts go away so I try and address them, not by recognising that it is my anxiety, but by confronting my partner to try and show them how it's made me feel. It is like not knowing the difference between being anxious and being unhappy. Thinking way back, I remember behaving like this a lot in other relationships that I have been in.

I feel like whatever the 'perfect' relationship looks like in my head is what I have obsessed over, which led to me reacting badly or not being able to take or understand certain actions (that weren't necessarily wrong) because it wasn't what I saw as being right. I would run things through my head again and again and as a result make myself feel really bad about myself and react to things poorly. A relationship is not like an injury: there are no boxes to tick, there shouldn't be an assessment of whether something should be that way or shouldn't be that way. But this is the part I have found hard. Was it linked to my OCD? I don't know. Was it those obsessive/intrusive thoughts going through my head, making me feel worthless and making me believe things that weren't true? Everyone is different and my way isn't necessarily everyone else's way.

Through reading this book you will have discovered that ever since I was a child, I have been anxious: anxious about wanting to do well or be better or whatever else. I feel that my reactions from feeling anxious meant that I cared a lot about doing well and meeting expectations. I have always had a problem with putting pressure on myself no matter what the situation, whether it's football, relationships or even simple everyday life.

I think the one that gets to me the most is how much it can affect my relationships. I am a perfectionist; I want things to be perfect and I'll do anything to make it as close to perfect as possible. Of course, nothing is perfect. What even is perfect? Exactly; it doesn't exist. But this is something I struggle with. So that's where the pressure comes in. I have very high expectations of myself which probably sounds normal for a sportsperson but it is not something that has helped me at all off the pitch. I will constantly over-think every situation, analyse every scenario as if the thoughts in my head are real.

So, when it comes to being in a relationship of course, it's not a healthy way to be, but you get so caught up in thinking and feeling you don't realise what's real and what's not. Not until you have to, I guess. Every thought has been thought, every feeling has been felt and you haven't really realised how it has affected yourself or someone else until it's too late.

It was always the same with my OCD, there were certain things I had to get people I was in a relationship with to do when it was triggered off or else I would be a mess, as you have read in the previous chapter. This probably doesn't make much sense to you as the reader but for me, little things like that meant my world would come falling down. I felt like I had let down the person I was in a relationship with, or I wasn't what they expected.

On the outside if you met me for the first time, I would probably come across quite confident, loud, funny, a little bit loose, some people say I'm nuts. Of course, these things are true, they are parts of my personality and that is me in a nutshell (from the outside) but we only see people for what they are on the outside or as far as they let you in. We have absolutely no idea what kind of thoughts are ticking through somebody's mind, whether they be floating through the mind or intrusive, uncomfortable thoughts. I tend to experience more intrusive uncomfortable thoughts. Even at the best of times they will still be trying to drag me down.

Everyone has been in relationships that haven't worked out, that is part of growing up. Further down the line as I have got older, I look back and feel that maybe those people just haven't been right for me. I would always blame myself for things when sometimes it just needed some understanding from that person; maybe they weren't in the right stage of their life to understand these types of issues. Which is fine: the relationship just probably needed to end sooner but because I was so obsessed with trying to fix things or make them perfect, I wasn't realising that it may just be the wrong person for me and I wasn't actually happy with them. It all came out in different forms.

Here is an example of what I am talking about. I already had self-worth issues and trust issues because of things that happened to me in the past. There was one situation where I felt the trust between my partner and me was damaged. I couldn't believe anything she said. Why couldn't I just be able to trust someone? I fell into a place where the majority of thoughts going through my head felt like poison. Any sense of happiness, I cut it off. She would try and reassure me, I would think of reasons why it wasn't true. It's like I had some sort of wall up that couldn't be broken down. This wasn't me. I didn't want to feel this way. I was killing my own happiness. Anything to do with her, I couldn't deal with, there was always something going through my head that resulted in me getting angry or feeling so low because of the way I felt about myself. Looking back, this partner wasn't the right person for me, but I continued to try and perfect things. There was no initial realisation that this situation wasn't right at all.

All I thought about is how I couldn't have been good enough which came down to my obsession with perfection. Even right now I am furious with myself when I try to explain how I felt about things and how the way I was thinking wasn't normal. Why would anyone want to be with someone like that? Why would anyone want to put up with that loser? I couldn't break out of how I was feeling, and I just kept getting more and more angry with myself because of it. I wanted to be in control of everything because I was so scared of getting hurt.

This was my headspace when I was completely blaming myself for everything —

My mum and dad tried to say 'Well maybe you need to be on your own,' or 'Maybe she's not the right person for you'. I would say, 'No, it's me.' If I stopped things and tried to get in a relationship with someone else, it would be the same. I have already had these issues in past relationships. It's the poisonous thoughts that I could not break away from. My head was toxic all the time. I couldn't get a break from it. I just wanted it to stop. I had a problem and I didn't know what to do, I didn't know how to deal with the things that were going through my head, so I ended up getting anxious because I didn't know how to handle it.

Now ...

It is crazy to think that all of this went on as I was growing up. This happens when you have relationships as a young person and this was a long time ago now; when you're older you realise that you just aren't compatible with everyone. I learned that after time on my own and being in other situations along the way. I always choose to learn from situations rather than ignore them or carry on in the same way. Whenever anything bad happens my choice is to analyse it and be aware of why I feel the way I do. I have become so much more self-aware and that has helped me a lot. I think it also helps when you value yourself and begin to know what you feel you need in a relationship. I have dealt with all sorts of people, some selfish, some unaware of themselves, and

I have sacrificed many things for others. It is important to understand yourself first before allowing certain situations to take over your happiness.

I am so much happier now, so much more mature in my head and I feel that has come down to learning from these relationships. There are many aspects to it: accepting people, making the effort to understand them, and communicating. In my opinion these must be actively done by both people for the strongest relationships to work.

Chapter Eight

Courage – from Crystal Palace to North Carolina

OCD AND anxiety issues have been with me for years, and while I struggled to deal with them, I was also trying to make progress in my football career.

In the summer of 2020, I decided to leave Reading FC. That decision was a difficult one. I had signed at the club on a two-year deal, and the first year – as you have already read – was when I had the stress fracture in my back.

In the second year, well that was when Covid hit. So, the season was forced to stop when the country went into lockdown. This was at a time when I was actually fit and injury-free and trying to compete for my place in the Reading team. Until then, my career had been so inconsistent, which had contributed to a lack of competitive game time. During lockdown I had time to consider my next move. I did have a call from my manager Kelly Chambers saying they would like me to go on loan for the next season, but I decided to leave Reading and join Leicester City instead.

Leicester were in the league below and had plans of achieving promotion in that next season. This challenge was appealing to me – I had numerous conversations with the manager about his visions for me and it all sounded exciting. All I cared about was increasing my competitive game time after missing so much. I just needed to play.

Unfortunately, my time at Leicester wasn't what I thought it would be. We did achieve promotion, but that 2020/21 season ended up being another difficult and frustrating year to add to the list, for many reasons. I didn't see a future at the club, so 2021 was another summer of looking elsewhere. Next stop, Crystal Palace.

The 2021/22 season at Crystal Palace was truly one of the better ones of my career, if not for football reasons, for learning and developing in other areas. It is ironic, in view of the place I was in mentally when I first signed for them in 2021. I was on the verge of quitting, convincing myself I couldn't do it anymore for many reasons. There was also the adjustment to training in the evening again instead of the daytime and putting in the work at difficult hours of the day wasn't easy. But that year opened opportunities for me that I have always thought about but never known how to achieve.

Due to having so much time in the day, I was able to focus on other things that are important to me, for example finishing this book! I got involved in jobs that I never would have even imagined doing, as I have always really had tunnel vision on being a professional footballer. This gave me the chance to escape from the football bubble regularly, which I found was healthy, especially when you have difficult times at football. As well as that, I am now so aware that my whole life is not about football, it is just what I do, it is a job, a career path. I have been way more switched on to my self-awareness and to the things I have gained during this experience.

During the 2021/22 season I met a lot of people that had an impact on me, positively. There are people I got to know on a personal level who helped me put things in perspective. Putting things into perspective is so key, it always is, and that is something I try to do often, although it is easy to lose track of this.

As well as finishing this book, talking to the publishers and working with my editor, other doors opened for me. I started to do work in schools with kids. I also got a job as a football marketing consultant for Sports Direct, working a couple of days a week, where I met many amazing people and got to work with various sporting brands. A lot of experience was gained.

Sports Direct hired me as someone who would help provide insight on women's football for the lead-up to the 2022 Euros tournament. They had a big campaign that came out before the tournament. It was a weird one for me, as part of my job was to research players: players I had played with, players I had played against. There were times I sat there staring at the screen, low-key laughing to myself while researching some of the best players in the country. Seeing what they had achieved at various ages, I found myself comparing my journey to theirs.

I ended up doing bits of media work surrounding the Euros and went to a lot of the games, live. The atmosphere surrounding the Euros was amazing: the number of fans who went to the games, the recognition and positivity around the women's game all increased. Seeing that is obviously exciting, not only for all the little girls who dream of being in that position one day, but for all the existing female footballers across the country. Witnessing England win the whole thing was incredible! The stadium just exploded and the celebrations after were unreal. If anything, it also helped me appreciate being able to do what I do and love.

In terms of my football career, when the end of the 2021/22 season came around, the stress and anxiety about whether or not I would get a new contract naturally began to kick in, but I was able to handle this situation better than I ever had. I tried to trust the process and control only what I could control. During this time, at the end of a playing contract, you get to reflect about what is important to you, where you see yourself and what you feel you need. I almost saw the season at Palace as a 'wonder year'. We finished the league in fourth place and that was way higher than we expected. I managed to show glimpses of the player I know I can be. I met people I felt were amazing, some that will be friends for life. The coaching was great but challenging at times. The whole year taught me a lot about myself (you will learn more about this in this book's Second Half), and I was able to do so much self-analysis and see that I had come a long way compared to seasons before. I went through some hard situations with my coach, but we always managed to work through it – well at least I thought we did. We had plenty of honest chats, which I do feel is imperative when playing elite sport. Some don't see things that way, but everyone is different, so you must be open-minded to everyone's approach to things.

Some of the conversations I'd had with my coach and manager during the season had been crazy; some of the things they said to me on a one-to-one basis had been eye-opening. It gave me confidence that they believed in me and could see something in me. My coach always said to think about the 'bigger picture' especially when I was disappointed that I hadn't started a game or didn't play my best. I have always made the mistake of taking other opinions too seriously and letting certain things stick. This is football and everything people say should be taken with a pinch of salt. That is a struggle of mine.

I was surprised when I had my end-of-season chats, and I did not get offered a contract at Crystal Palace. However, there was part of me that didn't really see myself at the club for the next season. Like I said, it had been a 'wonder year', and a lot was going to change, since their schedule was changing from the evening to the daytime. This meant a lot of the girls who played in the 2021/22 season wouldn't be able to continue playing there, as they have full-time jobs and there was no way Palace could match their incomes from those. That's another story, but it is such a shame that some women's clubs still have this struggle.

As the off-season starts ticking over and all you are left with are your thoughts, you never know what is around the corner.

On being told the news that I was being let go by Palace, it was interesting for me to see how I reacted. I compare myself to the way I used to be a lot, especially when similar situations arise that I have been through before. I think when I have been in this situation before, I have reacted on impulse, with instant anger or panic that I won't find another club, worrying about the loss of security and loss of certainty. The feeling of 'not being wanted'.

This time, I was at a point where I had become so open-minded compared to what I used to be, that the vision of seizing a new opportunity and getting into something different and fresh was actually really exciting to me.

It truly is refreshing when these things happen, it helps you understand that at times football can be very political. It is all based on opinion and not everybody's opinion is going to match up. Not every decision is going to make sense. Not every conversation is going to be truthful. I think that is why I felt fairly confused when I didn't get re-offered. I felt I had a good relationship with the staff and all the players, and I felt I contributed to lots of things and lots of the results. But again, that is football. There are a lot of things that go into a club deciding who to keep and who to let go and I do feel like you never really know the full truth behind the reasons in the end.

I felt the love from the players and the fans at Palace, they were always very complimentary. I had a fan come up to me after a game, telling me I was the best player to ever sign for the club (I wonder how many players he had said the same thing to). It is so nice to hear such things, but also very strange, that fans and coaches can think and say so many nice things but, in the end, sometimes they just don't add up. It puts you in one of those strange places in your head. It is a grey area, confusing, but we accept it and move on.

The result of a season's work turned out to be different to what I expected and that is why we should never expect; never have expectations because they will mess you up. The only things you can hold on to are reality and facts.

After the release from Palace, I had various chats with my agent and knew there was interest from some clubs, so I wasn't feeling too worried about finding a new contract. I was very relaxed, and this was a new feeling for me. I am noticing a change in myself. A change in my emotional intelligence, recognising, realising. It did help that I was on a month-long mindset course with elite performance coach Rob Blackburne (you will learn more about him in the Second Half). Almost everything he teaches is relevant and helpful to what I was going through at that time.

May 2022

It is a Tuesday evening; I have just got back from Ibiza with the football girls. I tried to contact my agent while I was away, but his response was 'go away, you're on holiday'. I mean, fair enough, I was meant to be enjoying some time off and not letting the worry of football creep in. Anyhow, I waited till I was back to give him a call for any potential updates on next season. I called during the day and didn't hear back. I hate it when he takes ages to reply: he knows this as well, it stresses me out!

I was watching TV with Mum and Dad, chilling, and Luca called me. I put it straight on speaker just so they could be kept in the loop with it all. He started by saying I had a deal lined up with a club, it was all ready to go through. He then went a bit silent. I anticipated what he was going to say: 'I have some exciting news...' I said, '...what, what is it?' He then said a few things, to almost build up some suspense, and went on to say something along the lines of 'I hear North Carolina is a beautiful part of the world.' My mouth dropped and I just said 'WHAT THE FUCK?!?!' I was shocked. My mum and dad seemed shocked as well. Dad was straight on Google before the call had even finished, searching up North Carolina Courage, an American team in the NWSL (National Women's Soccer League), one of the biggest stages in the world.

I didn't even know what to say. Playing in America is something I have always dreamed of, but the opportunity has been difficult to come by. This could be a once-in-a-lifetime chance, if it happened. I had always talked about playing abroad, I just never knew when it would happen. Could it happen? Will it happen? A million thoughts were going through my head. Family, friends, my relationship. What a mental phone call for a Tuesday night. Released by Crystal Palace, potentially moving to North Carolina. INSANE.

Now the wait for the actual decision started. A week went by after the initial phone call with my agent telling me about North Carolina Courage. There was another club interested in signing me and they were starting to get a bit impatient, needing an answer. As soon as that phone call with Luca had ended, I had automatically started to mentally prepare myself for moving to America. Not expecting it to happen but preparing in case it did. With that came that bit of hope that it really might happen. What a mental story that would be.

Does everything really happen for a reason?

I was in Paris with my girlfriend enjoying some more time off and I had a call with Luca. It turned out that North Carolina couldn't make a final decision quickly enough and because there was another club, London City, waiting for my decision, that forced me to agree terms with them and stay in the UK; I couldn't afford to wait any longer as I could have lost both options. I felt that maybe the time just wasn't right for me to go abroad.

Fast forward a few weeks, and I had started training with the new team, but no contract had been signed yet. I had decided I was going to be moving in with one of my team-mates who I have known since I was younger, Atlanta (whose family helped me with getting my first ACL surgery). I had been looking into finding a two-bedroom flat for us to live in while she was still away on camp with Jamaica. I went to view a flat and I felt it was the one for us to commit to: it was a decent price, and it wasn't far from training. I sent all the information but later she let me know that she was going to stay put in the same accommodation that she had been in last year. This meant that now I was in a new situation and was trying to find a one-bed flat or a studio.

I had informed my boss at Sports Direct, Fergus Barrie, and he said maybe there was something they could do to help with my situation, as at this point I was doing a lot of travelling, staying in Airbnbs and hotels. I think one week I slept in four different beds. I was beginning to feel stressed. He got back to me and said that the company would be able to pay for me to stay in a Premier Inn while I tried to find somewhere to live. What a massive relief that was. I made it my mission to try and look for my new place to live while staying there for the first week. I was unsuccessful and they paid for me to stay there for an extra week.

Meanwhile, behind the scenes, I still was yet to sign my contract with London City due to some miscommunication that occurred between the club and my agent, amongst other things. One day, when I was on my way out to training, I realised I had three missed calls from Luca. I thought that was a bit strange and told him I would call him back as soon as I was done on the pitch.

When I called him back, he told me that North Carolina was back on the table, and I was just like 'what the fuck, what is going on?' I would never have been in the situation to even think about going if there hadn't been any issues with the London City contract or if Atlanta hadn't decided to stay where she was living. I would have been tied into renting a flat and my contract would have been signed and set. I found that so bizarre, that all these things had happened, and this opportunity had come back. Is it meant to be? Will I ever get this opportunity again? Am I in this situation for a reason? Everything weirdly aligned.

Now the process of deciding had to start. I didn't want to let anyone down. I was about a month in with London City and a once-in-a-lifetime opportunity had presented itself. I think of myself as a good person, a respectful person, so I needed to deal with this in the best way possible: be honest and let people know what my thoughts are. Like I've said before, how is anyone meant to know how you feel if you don't tell them? It wasn't my fault that the contract was messed up and delayed. Nor was it my fault that the accommodation situation changed. It just all aligned at the perfect time.

All my family and close friends that I talked to about this option said the same things: you would be stupid not to go. You may never get this opportunity again. This is everything you have worked towards. If there were others in your position, they would go. And my own thoughts as well were that I felt deep down this was the right decision. So, I went with my gut – I decided to join North Carolina Courage. I felt like I was in the best place mentally that I could be, to dive into a challenge like this.

THE SECOND HALF

Introduction

I HAVE now told you my story, from my very earliest days as an energetic girl who loved football, through all my physical struggles with my many serious injuries, and my mental battles associated with anxiety and OCD, and my moves from club to club.

I have been through so many ups and downs, but now I am recognising a change in myself as I grow more aware of my thoughts. I feel happier, with my football career heading in the right direction and my mental and emotional health so much better.

I have worked hard to deal with my OCD and anxiety over the years. In recent times I have had the help of some excellent counsellors and experts, particularly Vernon Sankey from Improve My World and Rob Blackburne from The Footballer's Mindset.

My reason for writing this book was to admit how I had been feeling, admit that I have struggled, and to tell people about my difficulties in the hope of helping them cope with their own roller-coaster ride. I mostly want to let people know that this is normal, to go through all these things. So, in the Second Half I am going to share the learnings I have taken from life so far, and from Vernon and Rob, in the hope that it will help other people to look for the light at the end of their own tunnel.

Chapter Nine

Acceptance

VERNON SANKEY from Improve My World writes:

Millie and I first met in the autumn of 2018. It was in the Bisham Abbey National Sports Centre gym. At that time Millie played for Reading, and they trained at Bisham, where I also exercised.

The reason Millie was in the gym and not on the football field was because she was recovering from an injury (and not the first, as I came to appreciate!). I could see she was 'not in a good place' although she did manage a smile. The combination of these two factors attracted my attention. I asked what was wrong and why she seemed upset. I explained what I did, and we began to chat.

It was clear to me from the start, and regularly reinforced thereafter, that here was a woman of rare courage, resilience and determination with a big heart and, at the same time, a refreshing openness to new ideas and thoughts. She was clearly suffering physically as a result of her injury, but it became evident that her greater torment lay in her mind.

As we came to know each other better, she shared with me the history of several serious injuries she had experienced and the mental anguish that had accompanied them. She spoke of her own mental health issues and how they affected her behaviour and her relationships. We spoke about her relationships and the hurt she had experienced. We spoke about her football career. She explained how, at times, she would play wonderful football, score goals and feel exhilarated while, at other times, her mental issues would damage her ability to perform and cause her extreme stress and unhappiness.

As we came to know and trust each other, I began to introduce her to the principles and learnings of The Way – a series of philosophical and psychological practices that are explained in my book, *The Stairway to Happiness and The Way: Finding Peace in Turbulent Times*, which Millie read.

It is (some of) these principles and practices which I gradually explained to her in our counselling sessions and which she references so clearly in this chapter.

Millie listened actively and realised that she was benefitting from her learning but, even more significantly, saw that she would be able to help others through similar situations.

We discussed the fact that the main causes of stress and mental anxiety are all man-made and internally generated. External events are neutral. It is our perception of them that determines whether we live happily or unhappily, in peace or with anxiety. We create our own reality every day and our external world is a mirror of our internal emotional state. So, if we want to change the outside, we have to change inside first.

If we feel we are 'victims' of life, then life will reflect this back to us. In this state we feel lonely, abandoned, inadequate, insufficient and unhappy. We blame our environment for everything that happens to us, and our negative vibrations seek out negativity around us. Misery attracts misery. We have all been here at some time or another and it is not a nice place to be. This, however, is the place Millie was in after her several serious physical and mental difficulties.

If, on the other hand, we learn to rise above this victimhood – often through disaster leading to an 'awakening' – we can start to become 'victors' of life. Victors take charge and full responsibility for whatever happens. We are 100 per cent responsible for the quality of our life experience. It is up to us, and us alone, to decide whether to view life as a series of exciting adventures and learning opportunities or to blame fate (and everyone else) for our misfortune.

In the words of Helen Keller: 'Life is either an exciting adventure or nothing at all.'

Carl Jung said: 'Until you make the unconscious conscious, it will direct your life and you will call it fate.'

And Shakespeare said, in *Julius Caesar*: 'The fault, dear Brutus, is not in our stars but in ourselves ...'

As Millie began the transition from Victim to Victor, she also started asking better questions: questions about 'how do I learn to cope?' rather than 'why me?' This is the bridge from Victim to Victor and to recovery.

We explored many concepts related to this. We spoke about our obsession with wanting to 'control', to 'know', to be 'secure', to find 'certainty'. We explored the relationship between control and ego. We discussed how to manage ego and the importance of creating objectivity through quietly observing it. A maturing ego sees beyond itself into a wider, more complex, more complete, more inclusive world of possibilities and opportunities. It learns to 'let go' of its obsessions and traumas (OCD, and many other mental problems, are manifestations of ego trying feverishly and desperately to control what it cannot and driving itself crazy in the process!)

It also learns the importance of compassion, kindness, gratitude, generosity, forgiveness and 'acceptance'. By acceptance we do not mean accepting anything, especially bad behaviour or behaviour that violates our principles. We mean accepting that events happen. They are as they are. Life is. We need to learn to embrace and be intimate with all of life.

These were some of the concepts that Millie and I often discussed. It was a pleasure to be able to help in this little way and a real privilege to be so trusted and listened to. It is wonderful to witness Mille's growth and development. She has a brilliant future. I am very grateful.

We can all be in completely different worlds in terms of our thinking. I think one of the first things that I sort of started to accept with football is that everything is so out of my control in terms of injury (though in my personal life, when it came to relationships, it was a different story). When I got my last serious injury (the stress fracture in my back in 2018) I didn't seem to be as brought down by it as I had been by the other ones. Maybe it was because I had already faced worse injury news in the past and had subconsciously learned to deal with it better. I do remember feeling extremely grateful and 'lucky' to be in the position that I was though. I couldn't help but think about what could have happened if I had been in the hands of another club: would I have got the good treatment and scans that I needed if I hadn't been at Reading? There were moments of doubt and frustration which is a natural response to something not going the way we want it to, but for some reason I felt okay in myself when accepting that I was injured again.

For me it is so important to be grateful and appreciate where you are and what you have. With this feeling you can feel so much more positive about situations. The reality of it was that my body wasn't in the best state it could have been, having come back from an ACL and playing for a few months, not knowing a stress fracture was happening, but it can take a lot of time and a lot of effort before things start to fall into place. I began to realise this injury was an opportunity to get stronger and work on a lot of things in the gym to prepare me for my return to play. This is essentially what happened when I returned for pre-season with Reading (the second year of my contract); I had worked hard, travelled in to do sessions during the break as well to get me to the right place physically. But the emphasis was firmly on physically. Looking back, alongside the physical work I should have been doing the mindset work as well: putting things into practice, not just expecting things will be fine because you feel physically fit. You can have all the talent in the world, be the fittest you have ever been but if you haven't put the work in off the pitch on your mindset, those areas can keep creeping back in and continue to hold you back from progressing in the game.

Learning

I have realised a lot of things contribute to inner peace and happiness. These can be simple, such as changing your approach to things, changing the way you look at adversity. Ultimately the idea is to change your way of thinking and be able to observe your thoughts, which will lead to a much more positive response and reaction whether it be towards someone or towards a situation. During my football career so far, I have started to realise many things and I believe I have been helped along the way because of the challenges I have been faced with physically and mentally. It is important that we recognise these things, important that we recognise our struggle so we can learn and grow and ultimately understand.

Before I was aware of this deeper level of thinking I would look at my injuries, for example, with tremendous levels of anger and hate and frustration due to my lack of control over what was going on. I would say things like 'why me, I'm so unlucky' and so on. 'I'm never going to make it.' I was so caught up in the dream of getting to the absolute top level of football and things just wouldn't go my way. I tore my first ACL on 6 May 2012. In the following eight years, up to May 2020, I recovered from that injury, went pro at the age of 19, dislocated my shoulder twice, had surgery on the shoulder, tore my other ACL, recovered from that, and then had the stress fracture in my back.

That is by no means the way a footballer would plan on spending their career but it is these injuries that have helped me be able to see that I am not football. Football is not who I am, it is simply something I do and the mental struggle to come back from each of these injuries has helped me understand who I am and how to deal with adversity.

Similarly, the mental issues that I have faced (which also have relevance to football) have contributed massively towards my understanding of what really matters. It all started with the tremendous amounts of pressure I put on myself in near enough everything that I do – as you can tell, because I keep talking about it in most sections of the book. I have learned how to recognise a thought and see where it has come from and why it would make me feel so bad. I have learned that these thoughts are an illusion, which can cause a negative spiral which many people are sadly on.

We are not able to control everything that happens – we can plan but not all things go to plan and this is part of our learning and recognition. The plan can actually make us feel worse. If you believe the plan so deeply and feel real emotion towards this plan then when it doesn't come off it feels like the world has come crashing down.

Which leads me on to ego. Ego is something that really had an impact on my understanding. Many of us choose to blame other people for what is going wrong in our lives but refuse to look at ourselves. We don't tend to take much responsibility for things. I've learned that if we blame others then we allow the behaviour of others to dictate our feelings and emotions, instead of taking responsibility of our own. We need to realise that the imaginary fantasies we are attached to are not who we think we are. We need to have power over negative judgement and be able to observe these thoughts and turn them into a positive which will result in the individual being happier.

Acceptance is a key thing that helped me be able to overcome the storm of injuries I have faced. Acceptance seems to be something that some people find so hard to do: in some ways it makes you feel vulnerable, I suppose, which is something people are afraid of. Acceptance is dealing with the facts, not hating them. I spent a lot of time hating the fact that I was injured and dwelling on what had happened, rather than accepting what is and using my energy to face what was happening. It meant there was a huge amount of negativity towards everything I was doing.

There is a common theme: the more negative we are towards a situation, the more negativity will creep into everything we do. If we give off negative vibrations then negative vibrations is what we will get back. Amazingly this works with positivity as well, but this has a much greater effect as the result is a much happier and more productive approach, not anguish and hate. So, when you are injured and having to complete many physical exercises on a daily basis, completing the rehab is much more enjoyable once you have accepted what is, and this is something that admittedly took me a while. I have been in long stints of rehab where I have fallen into the habit of going through the motions rather than being present and grateful. This isn't an effective way to heal. It creates a negative perception and leads to unhappiness and low energy levels.

Here we are again talking about acceptance. It is something that we say all the time: you need to accept it and move on. But why is it one of the hardest things for the mind to do? In any situation the quicker you accept something, the quicker you can get on with doing what you need to do to move forward. I am guilty of trying to argue with reality, this is an argument that I will always lose. You cannot fight with what is. The truth is what happened, the truth is what is, not what we think it should have been or could have been. That is only a perception that we have created ourselves. The reality is, it is not going to go the way you want it to.

I am also guilty of expecting. Having expectations is a recipe for disaster. If you go into something in life expecting it to go well, you only line yourself up for a difficult journey when what you expected to happen doesn't happen. This is because you have created a scenario in your mind; you may have visualised how it might feel if the expectations come true. So, when it doesn't happen it is very difficult to get your head around and then comes the negative feelings and thoughts. If you accept it then the negative thoughts lose their power over you. Where there is no thought, there is no problem.

I have experienced many situations where I have got far too attached to a plan: a plan that I have created in my head and a plan that I would be emotionally invested in. My whole career for example has not gone 'to plan', which has led to many sleepless nights, many emotional breakdowns and heaps of disappointment. It has taken me many years to become so much more aware and I have had to take time to learn about lots of different things, look at situations in different ways, to realise that relying on an attachment to a plan is not the way forward. Trying to be in control of something that you cannot control is fighting a losing battle every single time. Saying something 'should' have happened is a perception of reality that is not true. Guess what? It didn't happen, so that is the reality for you.

I have been carrying the weight of my stories and issues with me throughout every opportunity I have been presented with. I have realised that this is weighing me down. Whether that be the trauma from mental stress because of injuries or not playing, or the serious trust and control issues in relationships, these stories from past trauma are weighing me down. Every new opportunity, I was viewing from a scarred past, scared and worried about what could go wrong. Always obsessing over the what ifs.

When you change the way you look at things, the things you look at change.

Chapter Ten

Toxic Thinking

Relationships

I have often found that being in a relationship is a pressurised and anxious place for me. This was due to my own issues, that I knew were there, but had not addressed and did not know how to deal with.

One of the things I have struggled with, like many people, is trust. Being hurt in the past causes a lot of pain for someone which then affects their ability to trust. The thought process goes something like: 'I got hurt, therefore I can't trust anyone, what's the point? I'll probably get hurt anyway, I must protect myself and take more control.'

But being unable to trust people just leads to more hurt – so it has the opposite effect to the one you are looking for, as I have learned. Having constant battles in your own head about ideas that may not be true uses up a lot of energy and ultimately results in unhappiness. The constant reassurance which I demand for my ego can almost become an obsession.

Obviously, every relationship I have been in has involved many happy times but on the whole what I have come to notice is when a relationship ends, I have a huge feeling of relief, like a weight has been lifted off my shoulders. Not because I was so happy to be away from that person, but because of the weight I carried in my head.

The mental offload was bizarre; I didn't have to worry about the most ridiculous things anymore, my OCD would seem calmer. Having to try and explain something like OCD to a partner is already a challenge, let alone everything else that would go through my head. I always tried to be as honest as possible and communicate everything, which was sometimes quite embarrassing for me as many of the thoughts were so ridiculous, but to me they were real.

When the relationship ended, the pressure I put on myself was released. The weight of the anxiety didn't weigh me down anymore.

Has the underlying issue been that the relationship wasn't right? I know a lot of this could come down to not finding the right person yet.

There have been so many occasions where I understood in my own head exactly why I was feeling angry with the person I was in a relationship with, but even when I knew they hadn't done anything wrong, I still couldn't stop myself from thinking like that, so the outcome was often the same. It is similar to the way in which I would listen to what my OCD wanted me to do even though I already knew there was no logical reason why, but the feeling of discomfort was too much to handle in that moment so the response would still be the same.

This was because I never took the time to actually do anything about what I was thinking. I never just let a thought come into my head, observed it and did nothing about it and let it go. Instead, I would let the thought come in, observe it, think about where it came from, feel emotion towards it as if it were real and still try to do something about it.

I have had moments when I would cry to my family because I didn't know why I was thinking and feeling in such a way that made me so unhappy. I didn't really see a way out of such thinking.

I have had to learn to change my way of thinking and that isn't an easy thing to achieve; it is something that will take a lot of time and effort to try and stick with.

There are so many factors that can contribute to why a relationship won't work but it starts with ourselves. There's no blaming the other person or other people for our own demons in our head. Our toxic thinking is ours and can only be changed by ourselves.

Uncertainty in football

Professional footballers experience constant change: moving from one club to another, building relationships with people, and starting again. During my period of transition from Leicester City to Crystal Palace in 2021, my anxiety/OCD got so bad that I couldn't even deal with myself anymore. I didn't know where to turn. What do you do when you have no idea why you're feeling a certain way? What do you do when you find yourself losing weight because you can't eat properly due to the horrible thoughts that are entering your head? When you have no motivation but you have to turn up to football and act like you care when all you want to do is curl up in a ball in bed? When you do not understand why the fuck your head is working the way it is in that moment?

My mum had to contact the doctor for me because I couldn't even speak down the phone to them. I was in such a state. I was prescribed Sertraline, an anti-depressant which is commonly used to help anxiety and OCD. I would have taken anything to feel a bit better at this point. I needed to get out of that pit.

So, I contacted an old counsellor of mine that I worked with many years ago for my OCD. What other choice did I have? To carry on like this? Fuck that, mate. This was enough, this was the final straw for me. I couldn't keep going on like this, I couldn't keep being caught out by it when I least expected it. It was now or never really.

It's not that easy to recognise and understand why we think the way we do, but once we start to observe our thoughts we can also start to observe where they are coming from.

As I have battled with my mental health problems, I have come to realise that changing the way I think about things is the key to being as happy as I can be. With the help of a few people along the way, I have learned:

- Only I am in control of how I respond to things that happen to me

- Suffering is optional and we can make it disappear by changing our thinking

- Everything and everyone in your life has a value of some kind.

Reflection and response

When you're left with your thoughts, you learn that only you can choose how you respond to things no matter how you're feeling, whether that be angry, sad, frustrated – whatever it may be. Ultimately you are in control of your own actions, you are in control of your response to everything. You cannot control what other people do but you can control what you do and that is one of the most powerful things that you can master in your life.

There is something that is said a lot in football and I am really starting to understand why: 'Don't get too high with the highs and don't get too low with the lows.' I have had to learn that I need to anchor myself and bring myself back down to earth when things are going well. Otherwise, I am focussing too much on the emotional side of the game. True power comes from taking control of these moments and accepting them for what they are, enjoying them when they happen but refocussing on continuing to move forward in that fashion. Recognising why it went well and believing that you can continue to do so.

One of the people who has helped me to change my way of thinking is Rob Blackburne, an elite performance coach and host of The Footballer's Mindset podcast. I contacted him on the recommendation of one of my coaches and after a few in-depth phone conversations, decided to join his accelerator programme. That meant working in a group and opening up about my psychological issues. Rob feels the group setting is beneficial because it makes you realise you are not the only one thinking the way you do. Everyone struggles, especially in football.

Rob Blackburne writes:

> I work with professional players on and off the pitch. When players are struggling off the pitch this often results in them losing form on the pitch. Football is 80 per cent psychological and 20 per cent football, so it astounds me that more players don't get help processing their thoughts. By only concentrating on the 20 per cent (the football) players are limiting their potential.
>
> Think about it, when you lose form, it isn't a skillset problem. You've spent many years practising your skills, they don't just disappear. It's a thinking problem, a mindset problem.

Mindset is such an abstract word. It means different things to everyone depending on their interpretation. For me mindset is this:

Your beliefs and assumptions that your behaviour conforms towards.

What you believe to be true, is what your behaviour will drive towards. For example, if you have the belief that the manager doesn't like you (a common problem among players), what happens? Your attitude changes, you become less motivated, you stop training so hard and next thing you know you're not in the team. All because you have a belief that the manager doesn't like you. How do you know this is true? How do you know they don't like you? Maybe their management style is their way of trying to motivate you, their communication skills aren't very good or they're going through a bad time at home and bringing it to work. You need to question your thoughts, perceptions and beliefs before you allow yourself to react based on them. Because the reality is, they may not be true.

This is where I come in. I am an elite performance coach who helps players work on their inner game. When I speak to players, I can figure out what their problems are and help them work on these. The brain runs everything so while players train their bodies it is vital that they also train their minds.

There are four main fears in football:

– The fear of failure
– The fear of judgement
– The fear of not meeting your expectations
– The fear of the unknown.

I give players tools to deal with these. As a participant in the group, Millie was vulnerable, honest and contributed a lot. Because of her enthusiasm and honesty, she actually became a leader to everyone else in the group. Millie is a joy to work with as she is so coachable and willing to learn, so she picked up on everything so quickly.

Not only did I teach her a lot but she also taught me a lot with her openness.

Suffering is optional

It doesn't seem to make sense to say our suffering is optional, but it is true that if we have the ability to change our thinking, our problems can disappear. We only suffer when we believe our thoughts.

The problem is, when a negative thought comes up, we go looking for evidence, we look for things that back it up. It is like some sort of police/detective movie that we create ourselves. When I don't know the facts or think I don't know the facts, I will go and look for answers that suit my thinking, for evidence that will back up my perception.

Have you been in a relationship when you think the other person might be cheating? What do you do? You start thinking up stories, I will emphasise the word stories. You might look at their phone while they're on it because you need evidence to back up what you're thinking.

This is a very stressful place to be. You are suffering and causing yourself stress and anxiety, all from a story you have created from a thought you held on to. Because of the way the thought made you feel, you have gone into protection mode. You think you need to jump to the conclusion of a story you have made up, or you need to prove that it is true. In this place, we should be the observer of the thought. We should question it and investigate the thought. It is a stressful thought that needs to be undone. Examine the thought: why am I judging this situation in this way?

Rob Blackburne writes:

> The only stress we can have comes from our thoughts. As we are right now, without our thoughts, we are fine. Our thoughts cause us to suffer, thoughts about the past or thoughts about the future. If we start thinking about the past it can cause us to feel anger, annoyance, disgust, guilt or shame and if we start thinking about the future we can feel fear, helplessness, worry, stress and tension. But in the present moment the only real negative thought we can feel is boredom.

This sounds crazy but think about it.

So, we have to aim to stay present. If you're stressing about something in the future it can never be true as it hasn't happened. Come back to now. If you're stressing about something that's happened in the past, ask yourself, what's the lesson? What are three positives? And then move forward. Here's a question for you. Without referring to your past, without your conditioning, who are you? You're just a being. No stories. This is where we have to practise being present.

Understanding and recognising value

This is something that comes to you in so many forms. Everything that happens to us is life trying to teach us something. We have to be aware enough to realise that and recognise what lessons can be learned from each situation life brings.

Everyone you meet comes into your life to teach you some sort of lesson that you can benefit from. It is only when you step back and view it as a teaching that you will realise this. You have the ability to learn from everything and everyone. The problem is sometimes those lessons are drowned out by our ego or it is made difficult to see because of the judgement in our own head.

The worst thing could happen to you but there is always a collateral beauty that can often be a struggle to see because we are focussing too much on the feelings and emotions that come with it.

It is incredibly difficult to accept that something is out of our control. We like to be in control but the truth is, you never are and never will be. So, the only thing we can take from these difficult situations is the teachings that come with it. When the mind is open enough to accept the lessons, the mind will become rich.

Chapter Eleven

No Rain, No Flower

FOR ME personally when I wake up and open the blind to see that it's raining, there is an automatic feeling of 'ugh, what a shit day'. I've always said I hate the rain. But again, this is a way of thinking. A preconceived idea that bad weather is negative.

Which got me thinking: no rain, no flower. If there is no rain, then there is no way for a plant to grow and eventually flower. Rain is a huge part of what enables a flower to blossom and grow. Obviously, this is part of nature. If you take away the rain then the growth cannot happen.

So, as humans, if we have no 'rain', we have no 'flower'. If we have no struggle, we have no learning, no teaching, no experience. If we only know about being rich, we can never understand the true value of many things. The rain is what grows the flower. The rain is what feeds the flower. My struggle (my rain) is what has made me who I am, it is what has taught me, grown me.

The weather is always changing, life is always changing. If it rained yesterday, who's to say it won't rain tomorrow? If something bad happened today, who's to say something bad won't happen tomorrow? But what we do know is, we are growing. We are being watered with experience, showered with lessons. It is only people who open their eyes to see what is, to understand what is, to live what is, who can see the beauty in a rainstorm, and the beauty in a life lesson no matter how cruel and difficult it may be.

I used to hate bad experiences, trauma, injuries, inconveniences, uncertainty, mistakes, OCD. All these things I used to absolutely detest. I used to say, 'Why me? I don't deserve this. It shouldn't be this way.'

All until one day it clicked, one day I could look back and see that every single one of these things has helped me understand who I am. Understanding life and so much more. Gratitude, appreciation. There is nothing to gain from fighting with reality, fighting with what is. There are only facts, only truth. And when you accept the truth then you will be unstoppable.

Ask yourself the question, how did I get here?

Do you ever have a moment to yourself and reflect?

Where you are today is a result of all the decisions you have made up until this point, all the challenges you have faced and dealt with or maybe still are dealing with. Every decision matters, every part matters; no matter how minor it may seem, it has all led you to this point.

Let's be real, most of us aren't where we want to be. We always want more. We always expect more from ourselves. But it's not too late. We always have the opportunity to keep rewriting our script. It might be frustrating when you don't accomplish what you expected to accomplish but the key word here is 'expect'.

Expectations will mess you up, so instead of expectations, have acceptance and be open-minded.

We all face unexpected setbacks in our lives, whether that be rejection, frustration or disappointment. When this happens, you need to ask yourself if you have given your all. If you're not careful, fear, doubt and worry will always leave you wishing your circumstances were better. You will get dragged down by the 'what ifs'.

It is important to separate feelings from performance and figure out how to pull yourself up. There will always be something to complain about, there will always be something you can worry about, but you just have to pursue your goal despite what is going on.

Rob Blackburne writes:

Happiness = Reality minus your expectations.

Think about it: what causes your stress? What causes you to be frustrated or angry?

Unmet expectations.

Unmet expectations of where we perceive we should be and how others should behave. If the pictures in our heads don't match up to reality, we end up fighting reality.

Here are some examples:

You believe you should be in the team; that the manager shouldn't have shouted at you; that you shouldn't have had that injury.

These are all unmet expectations that cause you to feel negative emotions.

We also have expectations of others and how they should behave or treat us.

A clue is in the language you use.

'Should' and 'shouldn't' aren't real.

For example:

'She should have picked me in the team.' (She didn't though, did she.)

'He shouldn't have subbed me.' (He did though, didn't he.)

'She should work on her passing more.' (She isn't though, is she.)

The biggest causes of stress are our expectations and our thoughts about them.

Get to acceptance as quickly as you can, so you can constantly move forward.

Remember, if you argue with reality, you lose, 100 per cent of the time.

A moment of stillness

There may come a time when you can just sit in silence and take everything in for what it is. At this moment, nothing is missing, you feel almost content. I have never been one for meditation but I'm guessing this is how you are supposed to feel while practising it. Nothing can hurt you; you are safe, you can focus on the exact thing you need/want to. Throughout life there are so many things that will change, so many experiences that will make you feel under pressure and things that will challenge you to the max and there are also so many opportunities to put things into perspective. The feelings and emotions we experience during these times are ones that prove we are alive. Alive and dancing the beautiful dance of life.

During the Covid pandemic lockdown in 2020, I experienced a moment of stillness, a moment of entire gratefulness that is kind of hard to explain. We were all stuck at home, at a time when positivity, hope and faith were something that the country needed to rely on and it amazed me how much a country could come together to support each other at such a horrendous time. It got me thinking. Why didn't we already have this level of support for one another? Our lives had all been turned upside down and some would deal with it better than others. It all came down to how we looked at it, how we decided to make the most of our 'normal' life being essentially put on hold.

I felt like I had almost stepped back from my life and was seeing it for what it was: absolutely amazing. I couldn't be more appreciative of everything that had happened to me in my (nearly) 24 years on this earth: everything that had contributed towards my learning about myself, the unbelievable highs and the lows that feel like a never-ending cycle.

Chapter Twelve

Me Versus Me

THE ONLY person you are in a battle with is yourself: meaning you against your head and the weight that carries. It's always been me against my head. I am fed up with fighting against my perception. It gets fucking boring. Life is hard, and the thing is you can deal with situations and better yourself, learn everything you can, take the time to get better. This will always put you in a better place to overcome the next level of adversity. Life is constant, until it is not, and we must know that things aren't always going to go the way we want them to. You never, ever know what is round the corner, what challenge is going to creep up on you. You may never be in the perfect position to deal with something straight away, no one is. But the work you do on yourself absolutely makes a difference to the initial view of the situation. The thought process can change the way you look at the entire event. Be rational, open-minded, accepting.

There's an intruder in my head

Imagine having a feeling of dread, danger and anxiety with you throughout the day. If you can imagine it, multiply that feeling by 100 and you might just start to understand what it feels like to suffer with obsessive-compulsive disorder.

For someone without OCD, it may still be difficult to fully understand how an insignificant thought has such power over a person, and it's not easy to explain, but OCD is an anxiety disorder, and such thoughts of fear or danger cause a huge increase in anxiety for the person affected, anxiety that remains high.

When I reflect on this whole thing, I feel like I am an absolute complete nutcase. But the more I write and the more I reflect, the more I understand myself and understand my thinking and the way I am as a person. I am an intensely feeling person in a crazy uncertain life. I feel everything around me so deeply, the highs and the lows are always extreme. I pay attention on purpose. I pay attention to detail so I can feel freely.

The deeper I dive into my issues the more I understand them. Doubt is a major characteristic of my OCD. The worse the perceived consequences of something are, the greater the fear of something bad happening, which causes me to want to do everything I can to prevent it. This is where doubt in OCD comes from and what drives a lot of compulsive behaviours.

In other terms, OCD demands black or white answers, it really struggles with grey areas. It can't handle uncertainty.

People that know me or have worked with me might be having an 'Ohhhhh, that's why' moment right now. This isn't an overnight thing for me; this is a lifetime thing. This is a constant. I can't predict what the future holds, I have no idea. This means when uncertain situations arise, I must try and tackle them as best I possibly can, usually with a boat-load of emotion.

This has been difficult, because as a footballer you are constantly judged for your actions and reactions. A lot of the time I suffer in silence because I know the potential consequences – especially when I am going through something that no one knows about. Anyone reading this that has been a manager or coach of mine, even a team-mate, I hope this helps you understand who I am. If only we could have this sort of information for every person and player. I know people struggle and suffer in silence. I want to take ownership of who I am. Nobody is perfect, we all require different things. Some more than others.

I am guilty of not being honest about the extent of my OCD, with workpeople and team-mates. I have always had the feeling people wouldn't understand. That they would see it as a weakness or that I was attention-seeking. Of course, there has been mention of OCD but not the extent of how it affects my life. I was taking anti-depressants for my whole season at Crystal Palace to help me regulate the chemicals in my brain. This isn't something I should be ashamed of, or anyone should be ashamed of. I didn't choose to have an anxious brain. No one would choose that. I wanted to help myself as best I could, but this leads me down the path of being afraid of relying on them. I want to be able to fight this on my own. I want to be able to control my emotions and thoughts on my own.

I must accept that this is a process, as is everything else: an incredibly hard process alongside trying to be a sportsperson at a high level.

In the past, I often felt trapped because I felt people did not understand when I reacted the way I did or showed obvious signs of over-thinking and obsessing over a situation that many people would just let go over their head. I feel like there have been many times when I have had to try and explain myself, which has probably got annoying, but I guess that was me just trying to have everything totally clear, black and white.

Some people say 'take it with a pinch of salt'. Goodness me, that used to be so hard for me to do because I obsessed over what people said too much. I remembered things, I held on to things, and it hindered me. It hindered my development on and off the pitch. Sometimes I just wanted to put my hands over my ears and scream 'FUCK OFF' to the constant flow of thoughts. I always say actions speak louder than words and when the two things did not add up (especially with someone I felt I had built trust with) I could not deal with it. I really struggled to get my head around it, to the point of my whole mood changing and emotions coming out because of it.

I may never get it completely right; my mind is a complex place. The fact that I know that and can recognise it when it happens means I am in a better place than I used to be, and in a better place than a lot of people who don't have a clue why they feel the way they do or why they think the way they do.

I think I am a hypocrite at times. Sometimes I ask myself how I can be writing this book when I can't even listen to my own advice? Why should I release a book to help people when at times I can't help myself? I am not perfect; I am far from it. But this is real life, these are real thoughts and real situations that people are living every single day. I owe it to my ten-year-old self. I owe it to whoever might be reading this. I don't care that I might get judged for what I am opening up about. There is no such thing as normal. But there is such a thing as happiness.

I think it is so important that you're careful who you share your information with: not everyone is going to try and help you. Not everyone is someone you can trust. Everyone wants to know your business. Everyone wants to get involved with gossip. I need to learn to protect my energy, protect my information. Especially in football, where you're in competition with people. I don't know what everyone's best interests are. I think the problem is, I am too naive. I know how I am as a person and how I am willing to help others and be a good person. Not everyone is necessarily the same.

Early in 2022, I called for a chat with my manager and coach because I had got myself in a place where my thoughts and emotions were taking over my body again. Long story short, we all know my career has been stop-start and inconsistent. Every season is an opportunity for me to be able to get that back on track, but I seriously struggle when I start feeling as though the tables have turned or people aren't being truthful with me. It is so hard when a coach is up and down with you, one minute singing your praises, and the next absolutely hammering you, and that is how I was feeling at that time.

During this chat, I said everything I felt I needed to say to the coach and manager, and then my manager went on to say what he had to say. Then came the coach. I could already sense how this conversation was going to go by the way he started talking. As soon as I sensed the aggression/anger in his voice I couldn't cope. I'm not one to just let someone speak to me like shit. If someone talks to me in a way I feel is calm and constructive then I'm all ears but if someone is coming across as hostile then I just can't handle it. I had allowed it to happen before, so this time I stood up for myself. He said things and I instantly disagreed. He then went on to say 'this is where I need to leave' and he got up and he left the room. I then got upset and tried to leave the room, but my manager stopped me and we continued to talk.

I just can't process things when it's so hot and cold. So opposite. I know this is out of my control but it still affects me massively.

Later, I left the training ground feeling a bit lost. I called my parents. The thing is, in these situations, who do you talk to? Parents are always biased towards their child and they are not in the situation, they don't see the day-to-day training life etc, so they can end up making you feel more heated than you did.

For example, when you receive the starting 11 news and realise you're not in it, it takes a minute to process the situation. Then you have team-mates texting you, saying they can't believe it or they didn't expect it. This is the sort of thing that riles you up even more because you can then see that others feel the same as you do, yet the decisions made around it don't marry up.

The reason I asked for the chat was because I hadn't started the last game. My manager told me my head was messing it up for me. What did that even mean? He also went on to say 'it's just football'. It's just football? Are you mad? For me it is never 'just football'. They are not in my head. They don't know my path, my story, why it means so much and why I am so passionate about doing well and trying to make my dream a reality. I carry the weight of all the bullshit, daily. Every decision, every goal. Every high, every low. The shit I have been through is carried with me, without fail. I need to finally learn to fucking let go. Let go of the past. Let go of the shit, that doesn't even exist anymore. The only thing that is real is this exact moment right now. The future does not exist, it is not here. The here and the now is what matters. There is no weight to be carried.

During the 2021/22 season I had already started getting help from Rob Blackburne, so this meeting with the coach and manager was one of the situations I talked to him about. I could just call Rob and talk about how the week had gone, how different chats had gone with staff etc. He would advise me and help me with dealing with the emotions surrounding the situations, and after getting that kind of ongoing help from him, I took part in his course in the off-season of 2022.

Rob Blackburne writes:

Football is an emotional game. We think we're logical creatures but the truth is that emotion runs the show. The best way to explain it is the Elephant and the Rider. A 75kg person is on top of a seven-ton elephant. The rider of the elephant believes he's in charge but the truth is the elephant can bolt at any time. The rider is the logical brain and the elephant is the emotional part of the brain. We need to train the rider to control the elephant and then make sure that the path for the elephant is clear (that's the environment around you). If we can train the rider, we can become more emotionally intelligent and self-aware so when things go wrong like they always do in football, or don't go the way we expect them to, we can be calm.

Most players say to me that they want to be in flow state or 'the zone': this is a place where you're working on automation without thinking about it. For instance, let's say I throw a ball at you, you watch it into your hand and catch it. You didn't think about doing it, you did it on automation.

Think of it like this: we have four 'TV channels' to choose from and we're flicking through these channels all the time:

External narrow – watching the ball come on to your foot
External broad – checking over your shoulders
Internal broad – analysing and planning
Internal narrow – solving a specific problem.

To play our best game we want to be staying predominantly in the external channels.

When we lose form, instead of working on automation we go internal and start analysing things that went wrong. So, when things are going wrong, can you change that channel from internal to external? If you can, you will go back to working on automation. This is why when you lose form it's a thinking problem and not a skillset problem. You know how to perform the skill, you just get stuck thinking about it rather than working on automation.

This is something I am very familiar with, letting the internal channels take over the external channels: constantly analysing which leads to becoming distracted from the task at hand (playing the game, or training). You must recognise the difference between what you can influence and what you can control. Anything you can't control, you need to get rid of thinking about it. We can only focus on the things we can control and most of the time it's your thoughts and perceptions, your attitude and how hard you work. Instead, we put all our work and focus into things we can't control, it is a waste of time and energy and leads to negativity, unhappiness and dissatisfaction.

Emotions are processed by many different areas of the brain; they are processed by a network of brain regions. I am no scientist, so I don't want to go into the technical terms used, but all the different regions have their own job during emotional processing and they all work together to identify and control an emotion. The more we know about how our brain develops and how it processes and regulates emotions, the more we can help with emotion-processing problems.

No matter how emotionally intelligent you are, you can still lose your temper, of course you can. Your emotions are still in charge.

Perfectionism is a weakness. Football is a game of mistakes; life is a game of mistakes.

Be yourself, do not let people manipulate you and change you. Be true to you. You can shift left and right slightly but if you notice yourself shifting too far left or too far right then you need to ground yourself, reflect and go back to you. If you are not you, you will not play the game like you know you can. We have our own natural abilities and natural ways that make us authentic. As long as you know you are being true to you then you will be at peace in the long run. If you are forced to be someone else it is only a matter of time until the weight of that drags you right down.

Chapter Thirteen

Brave Enough Not to Quit

ASK YOURSELF the question, how did I get here?

Do you ever have a moment to yourself and reflect?

Where you are today is a result of all the decisions you have made up until this point, all the challenges you have faced and dealt with or maybe still are dealing with. Every decision matters, every part matters however minor it may seem; it has all led you to this point.

Let's be real, most of us aren't where we want to be. We always want more. We always expect more from ourselves. But it's not too late, we always have the opportunity to keep rewriting our script. It might be frustrating when you don't accomplish what you expected to accomplish but that's where the key word comes up again.

Expect. Expectations will fuck you. We all face unexpected steps in our lives, whether that be rejection, frustration or disappointment, and we need to deal with each of those situations, and carry on.

We need to separate feelings from performance and figure out how to pull ourselves up. There will always be something to complain about, there will always be something you can worry about.

Pursue your goal despite what is going on. Have you given your all? If you're not careful, fear, doubt and worry will always leave you wishing your circumstances were better. Always leave you with what ifs.

The story never ends …

At the end of the First Half, I told you I had made the decision in the summer of 2022 to join North Carolina Courage in the NWSL (National Women's Soccer League).

The decision was made and the process of getting my visa began. Overall, I think it took about four weeks from when I signed the contract to when I actually climbed on board the aircraft and left London, maybe a little longer.

I quite liked the idea of being called an 'internationally recognised alien' by the US government – I thought that was cool! So, for those four weeks in August and September, it was just a waiting game for the alien. I needed to keep training so I contacted my old Reading FC coaches Phil and Kelly to see if it was okay for me to come in and train up until I left. They said yes, so I was in from that week onwards. It was a weird time, waiting in limbo. I felt a little stressed to be fair. I felt myself getting agitated when I was asked questions about when I was leaving as I didn't know the answers to them. I seemed a bit distant from people, but I know that was because I was subconsciously preparing myself for a move to a different country.

11 September 2022

I have just left my family at London Heathrow, Terminal Three. It feels like I have been waiting for this moment for a very long time. I have had time to mentally prepare myself for this, time to reflect over everything that has led me to this point. I am leaving everything I know behind to move somewhere I have never been before. Mental.

I am now on the plane to North Carolina. I feel strangely calm, weirdly okay. I am not used to this feeling. The complete unknown awaits me but fuck it. I am so ready for this challenge. I feel as though I am flying away from all the anxiety, adversity, confusion, bullshit. I am taking everything I have learned with me, and I am putting it straight into practice. Why wait? This is a life-changing opportunity. One I may never be offered again. This is the next chapter, this is the doorway I have been working for all this time. I have no idea what's going to happen, but I'm not scared, I am excited.

I want you, the reader, to be Brave Enough Not to Quit. I want to be proof of someone that was Brave Enough Not to Quit. To keep going no matter how loud the noise is in my head. No matter how shit the cards are that I have been dealt.

I have learned there are ways to get through what you are going through, but it all starts with you. Do not let yourself down. Do it for you, it is you versus you.

I look back on my journey so far and I think fuck me, how many times could I have stopped? How many times did I just want to run away but I didn't, I faced it. No matter how hard it was. I am still here, still living my dream and still learning, every single day.

Do not be defined by your struggle. Live your own dream and pay attention not just to where it takes you but how it gets you there.

Whatever happens when I get off this plane and enter this whole new world, all I know is I will be Brave Enough Not to Quit.

EXTRA TIME

Introduction

YOU MIGHT think I have had more than my fair share of difficulties and setbacks to cope with in my football career so far. However, every player will have problems of some sort that they need to work through.

Two of the famous footballers who I have worked with, Emile Heskey and Fran Kirby, have faced battles of their own, but were able to persevere and enjoy huge success as a result. They both agreed to share their experiences with me for this book, which I am extremely grateful for.

Here is my interview with former England player Emile Heskey. I worked with him when I was at Leicester City and got to know him well. He was a player mentor and ambassador while I was there, then, in 2021, he became head of women's football development and he stepped in to be interim manager of the women's team after Jonathan Morgan was sacked in November 2021.

Emile Heskey

Millie: I imagine mental health issues probably weren't talked about as much in the game back when you were playing as they are now.

Emile: Yes, especially in a male-dominated sport at that time, all the masculinity, you can't show any weakness, you can't do this, you can't do that. It was all BS to be honest.

With the issues you have had, were you putting the pressure on yourself, or was it coming from the coaches?

Millie: It was massively from within myself and the expectations I had. I still have them, but I can deal with it better now.

Initially it can come from a coach. Before you even arrive at a club, a coach can tell you things like 'you are going to be my star striker' and then you get there and there's other people to compete with and it's never as straightforward as that. If someone else is banging in the goals, I can't argue with that and it's about how you deal with that situation and I really struggled with it.

Emile: When a player's off-field problems spill into on-field problems you need to find a solution. As coaches, we might say 'you take time out' but they might not want time out, they want to play. Then it's a big hoo-hah and a tough time. Coaches need to be able to give players time off if they need it. We need that loving, personal touch, understanding someone.

Millie: Was racism a massive thing you had to deal with and something you took into your game?

Emile: Yes. You have got to grow a thick skin. You have got to work hard. You ask anyone from my era what was the one thing that their parents taught them growing up and it was [if you are black] you have to work twice as hard as white people to get anywhere near them. So, I always knew I had to work hard. That wasn't an issue.

In the 1980s it was fight or flight. I'm glad my kids are growing up in this era, where they can formally complain to someone about something. When I was a kid, you couldn't really complain about racism to a police officer. They would turn around and tell you, 'Well you *are* a black bastard so deal with it.'

If you were ever getting racial abuse, you either had to fight with people or just move on, take it on the chin. There were just two options.

I'll give you an example. I put it in my book. We played Stoke at home and as we were walking out, we were hearing the players saying, 'Don't let these black bastards beat us, blah, blah, blah.'

This started in the tunnel and five or ten minutes in they were still giving it. One of our players, a black lad, fouled one of their players. The guy goes, 'Oh you black bastard' and another guy came running towards him, hit the guy twice and he dropped. Now, he got done for violence or whatever it was, but I don't think he should have been done because we were 20 minutes into a game and someone has been racially abused from the beginning of it and the referee had had time to stop that and had chosen not to, and that was the consequence.

When the abuse came from fans and people like that, I thought 'you are not going to come and get me on the pitch, are you?', so I'm safe on the pitch. But in that era, when someone was racially abusing you like that, it meant they wanted to harm you. You had to be on your toes. Either fight or run.

You were safe on the pitch unless you were in local football, where it was proper fight or flight.

I was lucky enough to not ever be in that scenario, because I went professional at 16. I never had to deal with all that. I played in a football team that was all white, except for me and another lad. In that situation you are not really going to get racially abused. The abuse happens more when the majority of your team is black and you are going to play against a white team. I have friends and family who played in predominantly black teams and I never had to deal with half the stuff they tell me about.

Millie: Do you think that helped you in becoming so successful?

Emile: One hundred per cent it did. If I hadn't had that I could have easily fallen down and blamed something else, but it was 'no, I've got to get back up and go again, I've got to keep pushing' and that was the catalyst for a lot of people from our era.

I'm talking about an era when there was racial abuse, but if you go back even further, they were throwing bananas at players in professional stadiums. I look at my era and say it was watered down compared to what my parents had to deal with and what people like John Barnes had to deal with.

There will always be a part of that, whatever era you are in. It's a learned behaviour. A lot of our television doesn't help and we have had a prime minister who said derogatory things about certain people. It will always be there but we are hoping it will get a little bit better.

It definitely helped me be the person I am and keep fighting even when things are against you.

I went to Liverpool and did really well. Towards the end of my time at Liverpool I still had a year left on my contract and I could have stayed but I was told I wasn't going to play so that was the reason I left. I would more than happily fight for my place but if you are being told you aren't going to play, what's the point in staying? You move on.

The fascinating thing is, I went back down to Birmingham to build myself back up and I knew I was going to have to do that. It might be the fact I am thick-skinned, you just go and do it again and you thrive and you have no doubt.

I don't know how I got it or where I got it from but I never, ever doubted myself.

Millie: A coach once said you were too soft to make it, but you only heard it later down the line. Do you think that would have affected your path if you had heard it at the time?

Emile: I still would have pushed through. I had this ability – I still have it now – to hear people saying stuff and take whatever I needed to take in and let go of what I didn't need.

Millie: That's a skill I've struggled with. I have been taking too much on board and over-analysing too many things that coaches or managers say and letting it affect what I do on the pitch, when in reality it doesn't matter, it's all in your head. That's why it's so important players get the help now because there is so much being said and if you over-think things or have a mind that's anxious, or very active like mine has been, it's the difference between making it or not, and that's actually scary.

Everyone is individual and you can't treat everyone exactly the same because everyone's head works so differently. How important to the success of your career was the way coaches made you feel?

Emile: Massive, huge. But you've got to remember a lot of coaches are on their own journey and they are learning a lot of this. I didn't realise how much, especially in the women's game, until I got involved.

Gerard Houllier was brilliant. He was different in that he knew exactly who your parents were, so he would ask you about your parents, your sister, your kids, everything. He made you feel special. A lot of coaches don't really do that.

Some of the coaches I know in the women's game don't know half the girls' names. I say that's the first thing you've got to do, go and say good morning to everyone and make them feel like they are wanted around the place.

A good coach isn't necessarily the one at the side of the pitch, it is the one around the training ground, making everyone feel happy, making everyone feel wanted, making everyone feel loved.

Martin O'Neill did no training sessions. Zero. I'm not kidding you.

Millie: So he was like the player person?

Emile: Basically yes, he was the man-manager, managing everything. I kid you not. We would play on Saturday, you would probably see him Tuesday, because you have Wednesday off, so he would see us on Tuesday, and then you see him Friday. There were weeks when he came in a bit more, but most of the time that was his schedule.

He had this aura about him that people would run through a wall for him. He had good coaches – they weren't great coaches but they gained your respect and you just loved coming in to training.

Millie: That's what I've learned, that the environment that's created is so much more important than anything else.

Emile: It's more important than football.

Millie: Exactly. What's the point of playing if you're not happy? You play your best football when you are happy. It's everyone's dream job. People lose sight of what they've got. I find it bizarre.

In a team there can sometimes be a lot of drama and gossiping and things like that. That sort of thing spreads very quickly. Whether or not coaching staff are aware of it, players are aware of it and it does create a weird vibe.

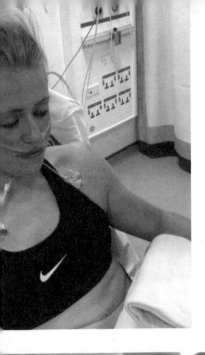
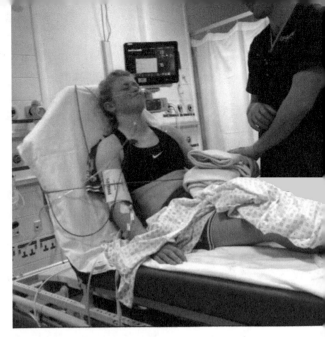

Second shoulder dislocation, in hospital getting it put back in

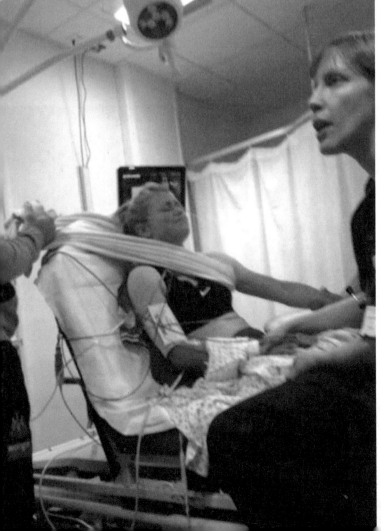

Scoring to help my team Bristol City secure promotion

Celebrating with my team

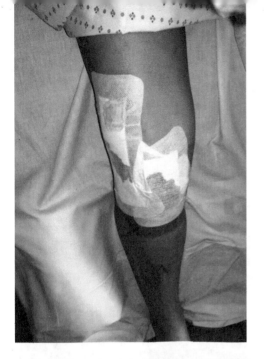
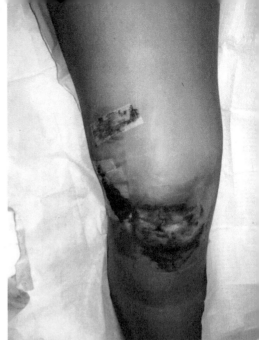

Post ACL surgery for the second time

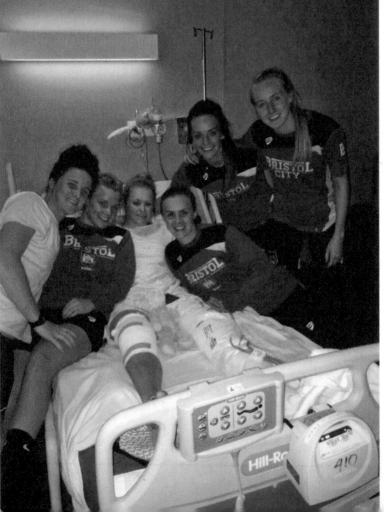

Team-mates visit me in hospital after my surgery

Bristol City warm up in Farrow 9 shirts

Reading

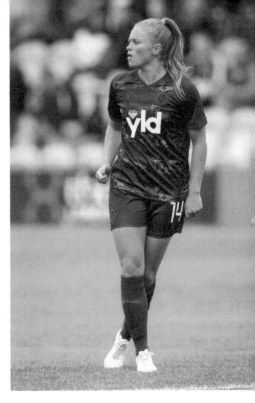

Reading

Getting treated for a cracked head playing for Bristol City

*Winning the league with
Leicester in 2021*

Champions 2021

2021/22 – scoring for my new club Crystal Palace

Celebrating scoring at Selhurst Park for Crystal Palace

A new journey begins with North Carolina Courage, 2022 NWSL

Then you've got players on the bench that probably didn't feel very important and that goes into the training sessions. It's all about mindset. That's why I'm so amazed a lot of clubs don't have links to psychologists and stuff like that because literally 90 per cent of the game is mindset.

Emile: If you believe you are the best player in the world you are going to inevitably become one of them.

Millie: And if you struggle and if you have all these different things that come into the equation, you are going to get to a point and then plateau.

When I came on and had a chance and I missed it, it was like my world would come crashing down. There was a massive wave of pressure and disappointment and embarrassment, like 'I'm a striker and I'm supposed to score goals' and I wasn't. How did you deal with missing chances, and the judgement from fans and things like that?

Emile: Judgement will come regardless. I look at it this way. Ronaldo misses just as many chances as you or me but he doesn't let it dwell, so he will be ready for the next chance, but you are not ready for the next chance because you are thinking about the last one. That was one of the main things I had to get over. I missed chances. I probably didn't miss as many chances as Ronaldo, but he gets more chances because he puts himself in that situation, whereas if you clam up and are like 'I don't want to go there now, I don't want to do that again, because it might happen again' – no, no, you are supposed to be putting yourself in that situation time and time again.

Millie: Apart from the racism side of it, did you ever experience any other off-pitch adversities that affected you on the pitch or did you take any mental weight on the pitch with you?

Emile: The toughest one is the attention that the sport gives you. I just wanted to play the game. I didn't care about all the BS that came with it. I just wanted to play football. I just wanted to get out on the pitch and enjoy myself.

I was a very quiet lad. I could be in a crowd and no one would know I was there. I was very, very quiet. But then you are thrown in this limelight. I had no media training, so you are not even taught how to speak, when to speak, etc, etc. You are tossed into the limelight and everyone is judging you off that. You are like 'can't you just judge me off what I do on the pitch, and not this?' That is the main part of it. But no, there's a package that comes with it and that is the toughest part. You are walking down the street and everyone wants a piece of you. I just want to go to Sainsburys, leave me alone. All that came with it and it was very, very tough.

They are dealing with it better now, where they are educating the kids a bit more. I did my first interview at 16 and no one had told me how to interview. I had the broadest Leicester accent you could imagine and everyone is kind of looking at you and going 'oh'. At 16 Wayne Rooney scores a fantastic goal, gets named young player of the year, he goes to the awards and his top button on his shirt is not done up and his tie is not done great and they criticise him in the papers. I thought 'hold on a minute, at 16 how were you tying your tie? How was your suit looking?' You've got these adults criticising a kid of 16. Let's talk about his football and why he's nominated for the best young player of the year.

This is where social media is quite bad now and the media was bad in my day; the media was the go-to and they used to batter you. The fascinating thing is, it's one fat guy talking about something that he can't do. Yet it bothers us. I'm like 'why am I letting someone else bother me, why am I letting someone else affect my day, affect my mood, affect my life?' You don't need to.

Millie: That's the right way to look at it. At the end of the day those people and their opinions are irrelevant. You are never going to escape opinions and judgement.

Emile: Ronaldo is arguably the best player in the world, but Messi fans will tell you he's shit. There are 100 million Messi fans who will tell you Ronaldo is shit, he's crap, he's rubbish.

When I was growing up, I played with Thierry Henry. Me and Thierry are the same age so we came up through our national teams at the same time, from 16 upwards, playing against each other. I remember the media criticising Thierry Henry and saying this and saying that, 'he never scores in the big games'. I'm looking at it thinking 'if Thierry Henry can get criticised why am I even bothered about what they've got to say about me?'

You've got to put things into perspective. Once you start putting things into perspective, these things are really irrelevant and you can move on with your life and you enjoy your life better. It is human nature to look at our social media and have 100 likes but there is that one person who has criticised you and you will focus on that one person and forget about the thousands that are being so supportive.

Millie: The negative has the bigger pull than the positive, doesn't it?

Emile: Yes. You need to move away from that.

Millie: It comes down to what you value. If you put things into perspective, when you are able to do that all that outside noise disappears. When you start to focus on other people's opinions and judgements that's where you get clouded and end up not being able to reach that next level or your potential.

Emile: The thing is you are allowing other people to stop you from reaching it.

Millie: It's a skill that we are not taught.

Emile: We are never taught that. I went from a 16-year-old just leaving school to having a camera thrust in my face, having never spoken about anything before, to having to articulate certain things in a certain way. Everyone's looking at you and going 'ergh' but let's see you at 16.

Even when I left to go to Liverpool, I was 22 and I was still a kid. My eldest now is 24 and yeah he's an adult, but he's still young. He still hasn't 'lived'.

Millie: That's where you get all that emotional intelligence. Life experience is what teaches you the most.

You didn't really get that many injuries, did you?

Emile: I did and I didn't. I got niggly injuries. From a very young age, I had a problem with having a big arch in my back – that's not good. It gave me really bad groin and hip flexor problems and back problems. My back would take over everything and it would go into spasms where I couldn't walk, I could only lie on the floor. In the end I had to go and see a specialist who ended up being the Leicester City physio for about 15 years, so I went to see him and he sorted me out and I had to manage my muscles and stretch them and strengthen them in the right way. I had to do that throughout my career.

I did my metatarsal when I was 31, I think, I did my meniscus when I was 31 and my medial when I was 34. I was fairly lucky. I looked after my body and exercised the right way.

It's difficult for women. Injuries are so high in the women's game. Has anyone done a study on why that is, has anyone done a study on what could prevent it? I don't think there's that much information about that at this moment in time.

Millie: There's a few people have done research on being on your period and links to ACL injuries. The hip alignment is different between men and women and the chances of you tearing your ACL while it's your time of the month are apparently higher, something to do with hormones that make your ligaments looser. With the women's game being at the level it is now and only continuing to go up, you'd think there'd be more scientific evidence.

Emile: I think there should be. I watched one of our players do a session last season and I was looking at her and I said 'are you okay?' and she said 'it's just a women's problem' and I said 'do you want to go in?' and she said 'no, I'll be alright. Call the doc and give me some tablets and I'll be fine.' I don't know what the pain is like but surely missing one day's training is not going to hurt you?

This player said says she knows her cycle and when is going to be the worst time and I was like, 'Why don't you just tell us and we can adjust everyone's training accordingly?' I'd rather a player missed training than be out for months.

Millie: She probably thinks if she misses training, she's less likely to start a game. It's that battle in your head, 'I don't want to say something because I want to play.' If there's a conversation where everyone's on the same page and understanding each other, it takes away that worry and that risk.

Emile: That's where the coaches have to be a bit more open. In one game, one of our players was sick but hadn't said anything beforehand and I had to pull her off and make a sub, and I said, 'You know what? You've got to tell me because I can only judge you on what I see on the pitch. I don't know what's going on with you. You should be telling me so I can protect you, because if you go on there and put on a shitty display, no one cares about the fact you are sick, no one knows you are sick anyway. They just look at the performance you've put in.'

I think it's a bit of both, the players need to tell and probably the coaches need to be a bit more open with it as well. Is that better with female coaches?

Millie: All the coaches and managers are on their own journey and everyone's at different stages and so many things aren't aligned and because there is so much movement in women's football with players it's hard to keep on top of so many individuals.

Emile: I thought we all had a good relationship at Leicester in the sense where I could sit and have a chat with you and a joke or be serious or whatever. When is a good time to sit and have a chat? Does the player call the coach or does the coach call the player? I don't know what is right.

Millie: From my point of view, the coaches and managers are seen as the authority. For players to be able to feel they are in a safe place to say anything, it has to come from the coach or the manager. I don't think you'd get a lot of players who would pull a coach or a manager aside and tell them 'I feel like shit' or 'I am really struggling with this'. It all comes down to honesty and being open and you can't really force that out of someone but if you give them the opportunity to talk, I think you would be surprised at how many people would. That's just my opinion. I am in a totally different head space than I was two years ago and more open and accepting of everything but four or five years ago I probably wouldn't have been as open as I am now. I have educated myself and grown as a person to get to that point of realising there is more to life than football.

Emile: I was lucky enough to play for 21 years. I was 38 when I retired and I've still got 50 years hopefully to live.

Millie: It's almost like it becomes everybody's identity, they fool themselves into thinking that is who they are where in reality, you don't know what's around the corner, it could be taken away at any point. You might not get offered a contract, you might get injured, and no one is prepared for that corner.

Everyone is too focussed on 'I want to play, I need to play' and they forget about their mental health, essentially.

Emile: What can the clubs do more when it comes to looking after the person?

Millie: Taking the time to get to know the players and that's where it gets tricky, because there are so many players. But if you have access to a psychologist and workshops and give players an opportunity to talk about things with each other or individually, I think you would be surprised about what does come up. I think it does take the right group of players to be able to do it as a team.

Emile: It's difficult when players are not playing, and they are not really team players, they are all about themselves. We had one player – I won't say who it is – but imagine you are playing and I am your competition in the squad and I keep going to you 'ah, you're not good enough to be playing'. This is what was happening.

Millie: That's the kind of personality you don't want in your team. It's good though that you are recognising that. For you, being new into women's football and being able to see these things going on, and coming from the game itself, you are almost like the perfect person to be in that position to be able to recruit the right sort of people.

Emile: You say the right sort of people, but you can sell yourself however you want to sell yourself. When you join a club, the reality is you are going to have competition.

I went to Liverpool knowing Robbie Fowler's there, and Michael Owen's there and Titi Camara's there, Eric Meijer is there, all these players are there and I'm like, 'Yeah, that's fine, what do you want me to do? This is what I'm about.' I went in and everyone said 'you know you're not going to play' and I said I'd work my way in – and then it wasn't a case of which two are going to play up front, it was who's going to play up front with Emile?

I am the only one that started every cup final.

Yet people will sit there and tell you, 'he's not as good as this player'.

You played at the highest level, Millie, and you had to come down to Leicester to try and build yourself back up to the highest level again. There's a standard that you needed to work to. I saw it with you when you had to do the running after the games. You were pissed off, but when you did it, you did it properly. Other people never do it properly and what does that say to me as a coach? It says more when I see that you are peed off but you are still going to put it in. You are never going to let me down.

Some people don't behave like professionals and when you go up to that elite level your attention to detail has to be even higher.

Millie: Absolutely. Is the missing part that mindset training? We are talking about players that have talent and have shown it but where's that gone? I feel that in myself as well. I want to get back to the old Millie Farrow, like I was when I was younger, growing up, banging in goals and I didn't care about anything. I just played my game and as I got older and I let anxiety take over because I didn't know how to deal with the mindset side of things, I ended up going down, down, down, and as a young player that's not where you need to be. You need to have that drive and ambition and motivation.

Emile: Until it's taken away from them, people don't realise what they've actually got.

Millie: That's what happened to me when I did my ACLs and things like that; I had moments where I sat and I was really able to appreciate what I had got and put stuff into perspective and when you come back you are absolutely raring to go and it's like letting a dog out of a cage, but if you don't have that inner bite, you self-sabotage.

Emile: Not everyone has that motivation to push themselves to go that extra yard and as coaches we have to drag that out of you. What you find with some players is that we understand them as coaches at the club, but in a different environment, like with England, they don't get that. They don't get the joking around. I love football to be fun but there's a serious part as well and when I ask you to do something, you have to do it.

Millie: It's getting that balance. Have a laugh and a joke, but when you need to switch it on you have to switch your focus. We are working now, not pissing about.

Emile: You've got to be able to manage that and I don't think some players understand that.

Millie: Well, I think I've taken up enough of your time now, Emile. It's been a very interesting chat. Thank you.

Fran Kirby

HERE IS my interview with Chelsea and England player Fran Kirby. We were team-mates at Chelsea and have remained friends ever since.

Fran has had huge success with Chelsea and England – most recently winning the Euros in the summer of 2022 – and has won lots of individual awards too. But she has had to fight some massive battles off the pitch. Her mum died when Fran was only 14, which is something anyone would find extremely difficult to deal with. In 2019 she was diagnosed with pericarditis (a painful heart condition) and missed many months of football while she tried to recover. Then, in February 2022 she began suffering extreme fatigue and exhaustion, which lasted through the spring. Somehow, she managed to be fit again in time to play for England at the Euros – an amazing achievement.

Millie: Writing this book, I want to help people understand that even professional athletes have struggled with things and been through life-changing events and potentially career-ending events but if you apply yourself properly and learn from all that you've been through, then you can end up achieving massive things, for example like you have throughout your career. So, congratulations on winning the Euros! It must feel so much better to have done that knowing how much you've had to go through to get to that point.

Fran: Thank you! Yeah, obviously it's a massive thing to win in anyone's career, regardless of what you have been through. Just to win it anyway is a really special feeling.

I think it was a lot of relief for me. I've played in numerous tournaments now and not got past the semi-final stages, so I think this tournament was kind of make or break if I'm honest. I think if I'd failed ...

If you get to a final and lose, that's just how it is, but not getting to that final, it hurts a lot and the way we had kind of gone out in previous semi-finals, it felt like we hadn't got to the level that we knew we had, and I think that made it harder, getting knocked out in those circumstances.

So, this time, to do it in England, in the way that we did, makes it so special, and like you said, with everything that happened ... not just in my life, but three months before, the Euros weren't in my mind. I didn't think I would be a part of it. When I got selected, I still didn't think I was going to play. I thought 'okay, great, she's taking me for my experience, maybe I can come on in the last 20 minutes and help the team'. That was kind of my thought process going in because I hadn't played football for three or four months.

To start every game, as a player my confidence was then really high because I knew the manager had that trust in me even though I hadn't played. She was like 'no, I need you in the team, I need you to be part of it' so with everything that's happened in my career and in my life, to just even be involved in it, it was really, really special.

Millie: I thought the same [before the tournament]. I was doing bits of work with Sports Direct in and around the Euros and leading up to it. They wanted me to help them choose the cast of the Sports Direct advert and I kept putting your name in and they were saying 'she's not playing at the moment' and I was like 'I know, but it's Fran, she's going to the Euros, she's going ... watch ... watch'. And then you did. That's the thing, you never know what's round the corner, even when you're going through something shit or an injury or an illness or whatever it might be off the pitch, you just never know what's going to happen next and I think for her [England manager Sarina Wiegman] to trust you with going in and starting every game when you hadn't played, that must have felt so good.

Fran: Yeah. Obviously, when the [extreme fatigue] illness first happened I didn't even think about it. I didn't think about going to the Euros or football in general. My life came to a standstill. It was like I can't think about football now, I have to think about being able to get out of bed. It was that extreme and then obviously I started to feel better. There were sponsorship deals that were on the table that got pulled, because they didn't think I was going to make it to the Euros, but that fuelled me even more to go, because it was like 'you are not putting that trust in me, the England manager can put that trust in me but you can't, then I'm going to show you I'm good to go'. It was always a question around 'can she sustain it? How is the fatigue going to be?' For me it was a way to prove people wrong – I'm still good enough to play for England, to play in a major tournament, even though I haven't played for that long. It was fuel for me as well.

Millie: It was almost like fighting two battles at the same time, fighting to win the Euros and fighting to prove people wrong. For me, for example, I've spent my whole career putting mental amounts of pressure on myself to prove myself, to managers, players, whoever it may be – maybe prove myself to myself. And a lot of the time that's had a negative effect on me, so it's interesting to hear how you've coped with that and how you turned that into the fuel that ended up leading you to win the Euros.

Fran: Yes, I think I'm very similar in that I have very high expectations of myself as a player, in terms of everything that I do I'm never really satisfied, and obviously like you said, it is a negative but it is also a positive because you know how good you can be.

Openly speaking, I think I've always been doubted as an England player. I think it's always been something that people have said, 'she never performs for England, she never gets the team going for England', so I always feel there's that constant battle for me anyway. So, I have to try to switch that focus and say 'you are here for a reason, every manager you've played with has trusted you, every manager has started you in big games', so I had to switch that narrative from 'all these people are saying things about me' to 'your team-mates trust you, the manager trusts you, the ones who see you every day on the pitch trust you', but it's not easy. It's hard to do something like that. I had to try and block out that noise.

Like I said earlier, I've always failed at semi-finals. I kind of felt like everyone thought I didn't help the team get to a final, so I was always a failure, and obviously I've been involved with the England team for a long time now, so there was more and more added pressure as time has gone on. If you think about what others think of you, that's just going to cause more negativity, so I think I just switched it to 'what do my team-mates think about me?' If you asked my team-mates, would they say they wanted me in the team? If the answer's no, then I know I am not at the level. So, I just tried to see it as how my team-mates see me and how the manager sees me, rather than everyone else.

Millie: I find your story especially inspirational. I feel like you've always been someone that people and younger girls have looked up to in football, but I don't think people realise the amount you've had to work through in your life to be able to continue your career in football. Back in the day, when I was at Chelsea, you suffered a few injuries and stuff like that. You don't need to talk about it if you're not comfortable with it, but the loss of your mum as well, that's a life-changing thing to happen and to be able to work through that and come back from the injuries alongside that, that's massively inspiring to people that may not know that.

When someone tears their ACL, people say 'oh shit, that's shit for them' but it's the nine months of recovery that people don't see that's the important part. And it's not just the injury, it's the mental strain that comes with it and the recovery.

Do you feel like there was a time in your career when you thought 'this is it, I don't know if I'm going to come back from this' or a time in your life when you genuinely thought you were lost or you had nowhere to turn?

Fran: Yeah. I always knew that injuries were part of the game. We put ourselves out on the pitch every day with the hope that we don't get injured. Anything can happen in a game of football. Like you said, when you were at Chelsea I had quite a few injuries – I had quite a nasty knee injury that wasn't diagnosed for a while. People see what you put out on the pitch for 90 minutes, they don't see the weeks of training that go into that, how you look after your body, they think that when you go home you are off out for dinner every night; they don't see everything you do in your life is to make you good at football. It's not like 'this is great, I'm a professional footballer, I finish training at three o'clock in the afternoon' ... I go home and I lay on the sofa. I'm not doing anything exciting because I know I have to rest in order to be able to give my best in the game on the weekend. Everything that we do is to prepare ourselves in the best way that we can. People don't see that side of it. They see the 90 minutes that you either play bad or you play good and they judge you based on that.

My mum passing away at the age that it happened was one of the two biggest changing factors in how I saw football. I took that break from football and I didn't know if I was going to come back and play. I was doing other things. I was training in terms of just running and gym work and I was like 'I love doing this, I love just going for a run' and I was getting happiness from that, not from football training.

Millie: You were only 14, weren't you?

Fran: Yes, 14, so it's probably the time where you need your mum. I mean, you always need your mum, regardless of how old you are, but it was that age where things were happening in my life, going through school, I was getting my dad to come with me to the shops and he would give me money to go in and buy underwear or buy tampons, and he just didn't have those things that a mum would have for her daughter at that age. I have so much respect and admiration for him now in terms of how he adjusted and how he became that mother figure as well, but that was one of the biggest things, like, 'Oh my God, football doesn't have a purpose for me anymore because I don't have the person there that was there the whole time. There's no purpose for me, I don't find it fun,' and I've always been a player that said as soon as I stop finding it fun, then I will stop. I don't want to see it as a job. It's something I enjoy doing and I love to do, so when that's gone, it's time for me to step back.

And probably the next big change was when I was diagnosed with pericarditis and that one, I really didn't know when I was going to get better. That was waking up every day, 'How bad are your chest pains today, how far can you walk today without getting out of breath?' Every day I was waking up going 'oh my God the chest pains haven't gone away yet' and that was one of the ones when I was like, 'I don't know when I'm going to feel better, when is this going to end?'

Millie: How did you cope with that mentally? Would you say you're someone that dwells on things? What helped you to be able to keep going and not let it defeat you?

Fran: I think the first few weeks I wasn't in a good place. There is nothing worse than having something taken away from you, in terms of football, and something really scary happening to you in terms of collapsing and being wired up by paramedics trying to find out what's wrong, going to a hospital and them saying 'we need you to stay in overnight because you are really poorly', so there was that trauma as well. I was feeling like crap, I would eat food and I'd have to be sick, it was so much anxiety and everything. The first few weeks I was not in a very good place at all. People would come round to see if I was okay and I would probably sit staring at the walls doing a puzzle while everyone else was behind me, having a good time and having dinner, and I just couldn't stop thinking about how poorly I felt. It was every day I was just sitting there thinking 'I feel so ill, why am I so ill?' and I couldn't switch off from feeling like that, instead of going 'oh look, people have come round to see you, let's put on a smile'. Normally that gives you a bit of energy to be around people but all the time, even when I was sat there having dinner, I was thinking 'I can't stop feeling this way, I don't know what's happening' and that probably lasted two or three months.

Millie: Did you talk to any psychologists or anyone that was able to give you advice and help you with that side of it, with where your head was at?

Fran: I spoke to our doctor a lot. He was such a great guy, every time if I needed to call him, he was there straight away and I confided in him a lot and he's probably seen me crying more than anyone has, in my whole career. He was the person who kept reassuring me. Even if I didn't feel it and I knew he was lying, every time I came to the training ground when I'd been away for a while he'd say 'oh you look better today' even if it wasn't true. He was always trying to make me feel better about my situation and put a smile on my face, saying 'ooh, you're not yellow today, you've got a little bit more colour in your face' or 'the bags under your eyes aren't as black today' so it was something to make me think 'oh, he said I look a bit better'. It wasn't like I sat down and told him how I was feeling all the time; he knew. He could just look at me and he knew. He would make comments and say 'you are going to get better, it's not going to last forever, you will get better'. It was difficult though because I hadn't heard of the illness, I hadn't heard of any player who had had it or anyone who had recovered from it, so it was tough.

One thing that I learned is people don't talk about things when things get better, they just talk about it when it's bad; that's the way it is, because people are looking for help when things are bad. I was searching everywhere to try and find a story where an athlete had had this and they've come back but people don't write about when they've come back, they write that they need help. So that's why I made such a big deal talking about it because so many people then reached out to me, saying 'how did you get over this, I'm going through it at the moment', and I was like, they can see that there's a story where someone actually gets better. That's what my thought process throughout it was.

Millie: If there's anything to take from it, the fact that you've been able to help other people in the same situation is massive.

Fran: Yeah, and I still have people now. I had two phone calls yesterday with people who are struggling with illnesses that I've had and that they are going through at the moment, so I am giving them advice on what supplements to take and what can they do in this time and what in that time. There are so many people who are struggling with it and you don't hear about it.

Millie: You've been at Chelsea for years now so you've formed a close relationship with Emma [Hayes, Chelsea manager] and all the staff there. How important do you think the relationship between managers and players is, and the level of communication, whether it be a deep conversation or not? Because I've been at quite a few different clubs, I've had to adjust to different people and different managers. Some managers don't want to hear it when you want to talk about stuff and some do, and I've found that me being honest and me trying to communicate where my head's at or whatever it might be, it always helps but not everybody sees it that way.

Fran: I think the problem is, when we think we show a sign of weakness, we think that is going to impact the selection process. Me and Emma have built this relationship now where first of all she can tell when I'm ill, she can look at me and know I'm not well, and then I've got to a place now where I'm not willing to put my health on the line. I've done that before and now I've got to a place where I want to – people will say it sounds dramatic but this is how I am – I want to be able to take my dog for a walk after I finish playing football, I want to be able to go to a gym and continue working out after football. So, if I feel that continuing the way that I am is going to have an effect on the life I have after football, then for me that isn't worth it. I am not willing to train and play that much that I can't enjoy what I have done in my career.

Millie: It's a short career anyway. A lot of athletes, not just in football, sacrifice so much that it does end up affecting their life after that sport or football.

Fran: I'm willing to sacrifice everything in terms of the controllable things, I'm willing to sacrifice going out on a certain day because I have a game three days later, I'm willing to sacrifice not going out for dinner. I'm willing to sacrifice those things, because that's what I signed up for, but I'm not willing to sacrifice not being able to walk 100m without feeling like I'm going to collapse. There is a boundary I have to get to!

Millie: With that illness [pericarditis] then, you still have it, right?

Fran: Well, I don't officially: when I have the scans there's nothing medically wrong with the heart.

Millie: But it's affected the way that you are?

Fran: Yes, I will never be the same again, I will never feel the same as I did before my heart problem. Doctors are saying 'your heart's fine', but I cannot train the way I did before. I have to be smart with my training – I can't load too much, I can't do everything that everyone else does, but I can train at a level and I can be fit enough to play, but if I'm not feeling 100 per cent I have to come out of training at the end. It's being smart. I am getting older, also, it's true! These things happen to you as you get older. So, there are a lot of factors and I don't think I'll ever feel the same, in terms of training and in terms of football, as I did five years ago. I've accepted that. I can still perform at a high level, that's not an issue for me, but I can't push my body the way I used to in terms of training and then going to the gym and doing another session. I can't do those things anymore.

Millie: A lot of the stories in the book are about me not being able to accept what's happening to me and being obsessed with a plan and things not going to plan and not being able to deal with it when it hasn't gone to plan. It's taken me a long time, and I've had to speak to a lot of people and learn a lot about myself and about life in general, to actually get to a point where you realise that until you accept something you are never going to get to that next level and deal with what is happening head-on. Would you say you've ever been in a situation where you've been going through something and you've found it so hard to accept, you've almost shut down and you don't believe anymore and you lose motivation and get stuck?

Fran: Yes, I think it happened to me in February. Because I'd obviously had my illness, I'd come back, I was the fittest

I'd ever been in my career, I'd pushed my body to limits I didn't know I even had. I'd had an amazing season, I was really, really proud of myself for coming back and then I broke down again. I had done everything I possibly could to be in a good place, to be fit, to be strong, to be good at what I'm doing and the body collapsed again.

Millie: In rehab you tick all the points, and then a problem comes creeping back, and it's like 'what the fuck am I supposed to do?'

Fran: Yeah, I just thought 'what's the point?'

Millie: How did you get through that?

Fran: I still think now I am a bit nervous about it happening again. I wouldn't say I'm completely satisfied with the fact that I feel better now. It's still always in the back of my mind.

I've probably made a decision with myself that if it happens again, I will have to rethink, if I'm honest, because I can't keep going through six months of feeling good, four months of feeling crap. It's not a lifestyle. But I always say to myself, 'Try one more time, do everything again, and see what happens.'

Millie: That's the athlete in you.

Fran: Yes, and the competitiveness as well. How much can you push yourself this time, how good can you be this year after last year? And I think I'll be really content with myself if I have a year where I feel really satisfied with what I did. So,

I think the competitiveness in me is 'try one more time' but I will get to the stage where I think 'I can't keep doing this.'

But it's not just me. I can't put my family through seeing me like that. I can't put them through coming round my house and I'm laying on my sofa and I can't move. I don't want them to see me like that either. It's everyone around you.

Millie: I get that. It doesn't just affect you. It's everyone else as well.

It's actually such a crazy story. You've achieved so much, won so many awards, you've nearly won everything and I know you said earlier about not being satisfied and always wanting to keep going and you have high expectations of yourself, but do you think that's ever negatively affected you or do you always find a way to find that inner grit to grind it out? In a team a lot of it comes down to team-mates and staff, all of those things factor into it.

Fran: I think when I finally finish football I will sit there and be like 'you know what, you did pretty good'. For me there's always other trophies I want to win, like the Champions League and the World Cup next year. I don't think I'll be really satisfied unless when I sit down afterwards, I've won those things, but even if I don't, I will still say 'you know what, you did alright, everything that you went through, you did pretty good'.

Millie: Pretty good Fran, pretty good!

What do you think is the main thing you've learned about yourself along the way, not from the winning and the achievements, but from going through that adversity alongside it?

Fran: I think the biggest thing I learned is the resilience part of it, how much you can go through and still push yourself to the limits. I'm in the very fortunate position that I get to do the job I love every day and maybe people who go through similar things and they are in a position where they don't love what they do, maybe they don't have that drive. I understand how fortunate I am that I get to work with some of the best people in the country medically, football-wise and business-wise. I'm very fortunate, but I think to be able to go through the things I did shows even when I get knocked down, I have that drive and competitiveness to say 'do you know what? No. Come on, one more time', like I said. In fact, it's not one more time – I've tried three times – but I always say to myself 'one more' and it just shows how driven I am, to succeed and to give everything to something that I love.

I think as well, off the pitch I've learned the importance of speaking up and telling stories, and I have always been an advocate for … we are all human beings as well, we are not just footballers, we are human beings and we have emotions, we have feelings, we have things that happen in our lives. People expect footballers now to lose a family member and go and play the next day. It's not normal.

Millie: No, we're not robots.

Fran: For me that's always been the biggest thing. When it came out about my problems that I had in February, people were like 'oh she's just tired' but you don't understand what we put our bodies through every day. People just see the 90 minutes, like you said earlier, they don't see everything else going on. You go and ask my team-mates 'how was Fran during that period?' They were like 'Jesus Christ'. Lauren James looked at me and was like 'you look like you are going to die' it was that extreme.

Millie: For God's sake!

Fran: I was like, 'that's great, thanks!'

Millie: I won't keep you for much longer. One more question and that will be it. What would you say to the younger generation of girls that eventually want to end up being in your place one day? What sort of words of wisdom do you have for that little ten-year-old who might have just lost someone or is going through an injury and they think they are going to give up? What would you say to them? Or even to you as a 14-year-old?

Fran: It's funny when I get asked this question because you can say all the things in terms of 'it will be worth it' and 'everything works out in the end' and they do, or it won't, and it's one or the other. I always think more of emotions. For me, if I could say anything to my 14-year-old self, it would probably be 'get ready, this is going to be a journey, it's going to be a tough ride, it's going to be full of amazing times, it's going to be full of sad times, emotional times, hard times' and I think it would be very much to 'try and find the balance, try and find a happy medium, try and find what makes you at peace'. Because you can talk about performance and people coming back from injuries but I think the hardest thing for me during my career has been me dealing with my emotions. When I lose a game, when I win a game, how do I deal with the emotions? How do I deal with losing a Champions League Final? Going from winning the league the week before, being on cloud nine, to losing a Champions League Final. And then, by the way, you've got to get ready for an Olympics. And then, by the way, you are going to get injured two days before the Olympics and maybe not make the team. It's ...

Millie: Honestly, you never know what's round the corner, do you?

Fran: No, you don't.

Millie: It's about trying to get to that place where, you are never ready but you can be at least a little bit prepared for what might happen.

Fran: Yeah, exactly and if you can mentally deal with it, deal with the highs, deal with the lows, then you are already on to a winner.

Millie: What a great conversation that was. Thank you so much.

Acknowledgements

I WOULD like to thank everyone who has been involved in making this book happen, starting with Pitch Publishing, thank you for allowing me to bring my vision to life. Thank you to Katie Field, my editor, for working closely with me during this process to turn my story and everything I have learned into a book.

Mum, Dad, Ollie and Eden – I want to thank you for the unconditional love and support through everything. I genuinely wouldn't be where I am without you all, you are my inspiration. I would also like to thank my mum and dad for the time they have dedicated since I was young, the encouragement and belief in me to pursue my dream even through the worst of times.

Big thanks go to Emile Heskey and Fran Kirby for sharing their unique experiences and honest words.

Thank you to Vernon Sankey (from Improve My World) and Rob Blackburne (from The Footballer's Mindset) for being instrumental in helping me change my mindset and contributing massively to my learning, and for taking the time to add their thoughts to my writing.

I want to thank my friends, my team-mates, coaches, managers and my agency, who have all been part of my career/life so far. You have all played a huge part in my realisations.

To everyone who saw something in me and gave me opportunities, I will be forever grateful.